Your Faith Affects Your Family

Volume 2

A Bible Study for Women

Ruth Ann Larkly

Your Faith Affects Your Family, Volume 2
Copyright © 2012 by Ruth Ann Larkly

Feel free to contact Ruth Ann Larkly at rlarkly@juno.com for any orders, comments, or additional information.

All Scripture references are taken from the King James Version.

Printed in USA

ISBN 978-0-9859895-1-4

Dedication

To Sandy Wilhelm—my mother.
Thank you for being a virtuous woman.
Your faith has had such a positive influence
in my life and our family.
We love you!

To Tim Larkly—my husband and best friend.
Thank you for being a spiritual leader
in our home. Your love for the Lord
has strengthened my faith in Him.
I love you!

Acknowledgements

This second volume could not have been finished without the help of many people. Thank you so much for the time, energy, and prayers you have invested into this book.

First of all, to God be the glory. He wanted me to write this second volume, and it is His grace that has enabled me to complete this study. Thank You, Lord, for always keeping Your promises.

To Tim Larkly—my husband and editor. Thank you for doing the cover design and layout of this book. It looks great! Your support in this study has been invaluable.

To Harry and Carol Hix—my faithful proofreaders and wise counselors. Thank you for the endless hours you have poured into this book. Your wise advice to my seemingly endless questions has been such a help to me.

To Ed and Sandy Wilhelm—my parents. Thank you for your prayer support. And thanks, Mom, for your help with the proofreading.

To Grace Hardy—my spiritual mentor. Thank you for the great idea of making the Bible study into two volumes. You have always been so encouraging of this project.

To all my readers of Volume 1—Thank you for the encouraging e-mails, phone calls, cards, and orders. Your response has humbled me and encouraged me to press on in this study.

And to you—my reader. Thank you for taking the time to read this Bible study. It is my desire that this study will strengthen you in your faith, ultimately strengthening your family.

Table of Contents

Introduction

When my oldest daughter was a little over a year old, the Lord impressed upon my heart to write a Bible study about women from the Bible whose faith affected their families. I wrote about these women with just a pen and notebook; and the more I studied, the more convinced I was that my faith would affect my family. That thought really convicted me, and my Bible study began to change my life.

The most life-changing decision you will ever make is to ask Jesus Christ into your heart to be your personal Savior. If you are not saved, I beg you to ask Him to be your Savior. Located in the back of this book is a section called "God's Plan of Salvation." Not only read through the verses, but also believe in Him and call upon Him today. Your decision to become a born-again Christian will affect your future and hopefully many others, as well.

Because the Bible has much to say about how one life can powerfully influence another, I collected quite a few women in my collection. At the advice of Grace Hardy, I picked twelve to go in the first volume and reserved twelve others for this second volume. Organized like Volume 1, this study is comprised of twelve women whose faith affected their families—either positively or negatively.

It is my prayer that as you go through this Bible study, you will realize how influential your life is and strive to be a woman of faith. May God bless you and your family!

Chapter One

Widow of a College Student
A Woman Who Went to God When Facing Troubles
2 Kings 4:1-7

Scenario 1:

"Hi, Susan. I was wondering if you could help me with some problems I have."

"Oh, sure, Linda. What's up?"

"Well, it's more like everything is down. I lost my job, the kids are getting out of hand, and my husband isn't very involved in our family anymore."

"I know that about your husband. He makes you do everything. I'm glad you came to me for advice. What you need is to pursue your own career. Why should you be the one stuck doing everything for the family? He needs to know you have your own life, too. At church tomorrow, I'll introduce you to someone who's been in your situation. She has a daycare in her home and will be able to watch your kids while you take classes from the college."

"You know, you're right. I've always put my family's needs first, but it's time I did something for me. Thanks for the good advice. I'm so glad I came to you for help."

Scenario 2:

Abigail gets on her computer. She is mad at some things her husband has done but doesn't know what to do. She logs into a Christian chat room, asking "godly" people (she has no idea who they are) for

7

helpful advice. The "godly" people advise her to separate from her husband and "find out who she is" by starting her own career.

What's wrong with the above scenarios? These ladies are going to the wrong source for help. Both ladies are Christians, but they are not seeking the Lord for help. Though these stories are fictional, unfortunately, the scenarios are too true.

The question is not "if" we will ever have troubles but "when." Nobody is exempt from having troubles in life. The real question is, "Who do you turn to for help?" Is God the first person on your list you call or the third? Look at what God says He will do if you call upon Him. "He shall call upon me, and I will answer him: I will be with him in trouble; I will deliver him, and honour him" (Ps. 91:15).

When facing troublesome times, a widow lady whose husband had been enrolled in Elisha's college went to Elisha, the man of God. During those Bible times, when you went to a prophet for help, it was as if you went straight to God. We should learn to go straight to God when troubles come.

Being in Debt

Her husband was a college student at Elisha's school of prophets (2 Kings 4:1). Like other college students, this couple struggled financially. Having two sons made provisions for food scarce. Soon, the parents made some unwise financial choices and found themselves deep in debt. They borrowed from a man called a creditor, who was probably only too happy to "help" this couple.

What a sorrowful day it was for the wife and her two sons when her husband died. Making the funeral arrangements had been tough, but even tougher was the day the creditor showed up. He informed the wife that he wanted to be paid; otherwise, for payment he would take her two sons as slaves. Can you imagine the panic that flew into her heart? She hurried home and sold everything she had. However, she knew that she still owed plenty more money.

8

Being in debt is a horrible place to be. And when your debt causes your family to suffer, it makes your financial situation even worse. In most cases, debt will affect not only those who accumulated it but also the whole family.

I am not a financial guru, but I do understand some things about money. If you do not get your money situation under control, it will control you. "No man can serve two masters: for either he will hate the one, and love the other; or else he will hold to the one, and despise the other. Ye cannot serve God and mammon" (Matt. 6:24). When you are in debt, you will be the slave and the money will be your master. When your financial decisions are all based around money instead of God's plan, money is your master.

There are two ways to get out of debt: spend less than you make or make more than you spend. Help your husband with the finances by learning to be content with what you have and thrifty with your resources. Be informed about your financial situation. Do you know how much your gas bill runs every month? Do you know how much your mortgage is and when it is due? Read a book or listen to a book on CD about money. Learn the difference between an asset and a liability. Study the Bible and see what God says about tithing. Communicate with your husband about the family's finances. Pray for a creative way to make money. Play an active role in helping your family get out of debt and having a successful financial future.

Asking Wise Counsel from the Man of God

After having lost her husband, the widow certainly didn't want to lose her two sons. Because there were no jobs available to females back then, she had few options. She decided the best thing was to go see the prophet Elisha. She cried unto him, "Thy servant my husband is dead; and thou knowest that thy servant did fear the LORD: and the creditor is come to take unto him my two sons to be bondmen" (2 Kings 4:1). She reminded Elisha that her husband had been a servant and feared the Lord; he wasn't just some bum who squandered away the family's money.

Elisha asked her, "What shall I do for thee? tell me, what hast thou in the house?" Elisha wanted to find out what assets (things that could bring her money) she had in her house. Perhaps he also wanted to see if she had sold her goods.

She said, "Thine handmaid hath not any thing in the house, save a pot of oil" (2 Kings 4:2). The oil she had left was "literally, save an anointing of oil; i.e. so much oil as will suffice for one anointing of my person."[1] Her only item left in the house was just enough oil to cover a body once. That was it—it wasn't very much. Thankfully, the man of God had a plan that would help her. Seeking counsel from the man of God was a wise decision.

It takes humility to go to the man of God and admit you need counsel, but don't let your pride cause you from making a mistake that could affect others. "Where no counsel is, the people fall: but in the multitude of counsellers there is safety" (Prov. 11:14).

Thoughts on receiving counsel from the man of God: First of all, pray that you will have a listening heart. Go with the attitude of fully listening and doing what he suggests. Don't go with the attitude of just picking and choosing things he says you should do, but do all he suggests. Too often we have our minds made up before we even receive counsel as to what we should do, and our hearts and minds are not prepared for anyone's advice. Secondly, be honest. Don't hold back important information, for this could change his advice. Thirdly, be open to changing things God may nudge you to work on. Don't focus on how you can change your situation or other people. Be open to doing what God may want you to do and open to learning what God may want you to learn.

A wise person will listen to wise counsel. "The way of a fool is right in his own eyes: but he that hearkeneth unto counsel is wise" (Prov. 12:15). Who better to go to for advice than your pastor, the man of God? Stay away from ungodly counsel (Ps. 1:1), and cling to the counsel of the man of God.

Having Faith God Would Increase the Little She Had

Elisha replied, "Go, borrow thee vessels abroad of all thy neighbours, even empty vessels; borrow not a few. And when thou art come in, thou shalt shut the door upon thee and upon thy sons, and shalt pour out into all those vessels, and thou shalt set aside that which is full" (2 Kings 4:3-4).

Because she was in debt, the last thing in the world she probably wanted to do was borrow! And now she needs to borrow pots from her neighbors! Her pride could have held her back from listening and obeying, but instead she humbly left Elisha to start working on the plan.

She hurried home to take action. Gathering her two sons together, she informed them of their enormous task. Informing them the importance of their mission, she made sure they understood they must ask all their neighbors for pots (she probably wished she could have skipped a few neighbors!). Her faith that God would increase her oil sprung her and her boys into action.

When you give God a little of something, and it's all you have, He can increase it beyond your wildest dreams. God can take something little and make it something big, thus increasing it. He can take a talent you may be using for Him that you aren't very talented in and increase it.

I know there are several things I am not talented in; but because I do them for the Lord, He has increased them. "The oil was to be multiplied in pouring…The way to increase what we have is to use it; to him that so hath shall be given. It is not hoarding the talents, but trading with them, that doubles them."[2]

Jesus increased the little lunch the boy gave to Him (John 6:13). The power of the Holy Spirit increased the word of God and believers in the first church of Jerusalem (Acts 6:7). The apostle Paul and Apollos spread the good news of the gospel, "but God gave the increase" (1 Cor. 3:6).

In order for God to increase what you have, you must make sure you give Him something to increase. For example, if you want to be a

11

pianist for the church, make sure you are practicing and learning about the piano. You will not just wake up one day and know how to play for the congregation and choir. When you give your little bit, and it's all you have, that is when faith comes into the picture. Let God take what you have, and by faith let Him increase it.

Under the Helping Hand of God

"So she went from him, and shut the door upon her and upon her sons, who brought the vessels to her; and she poured out" (2 Kings 4:5). Can you imagine the scene as she and her two sons knocked on their neighbors' doors, asking for pots? They had to carefully carry the pots and keep track of whose pots belonged to whom. After closing the door behind her and her two sons, she took her one serving of oil. One of her sons brought her a pot, and she carefully poured the oil into the pot. After it filled all the way to the brim, the second son had the second pot ready. She poured, filled, got another pot...poured, filled, got another pot. It was amazing! The oil never dried up.

"And it came to pass, when the vessels were full, that she said unto her son, Bring me yet a vessel. And he said unto her, There is not a vessel more. And the oil stayed" (2 Kings 4:6). Every pot they had was full of oil.

To put this into a modern day perspective, think of the oil as gold. If you were in debt, wouldn't you love to have pots of gold all over your house? The oil was very valuable at this time. "Because of its many uses, it was much in demand. If one had olive oil to sell, it would not be difficult to market."[3]

Rejoicing at all the oil in her house, she realized she didn't know what to do next. She went to the man of God a second time, excitedly telling him about her miracle. "And he said, Go, sell the oil, and pay thy debt, and live thou and thy children of the rest" (2 Kings 4:7).

Her job was not finished yet. After figuring out a way to transport the oil to the market, she had to sell it. She had to wash the oil out of the pots she borrowed, transport them back home, and return them

12

to all her neighbors. I'm sure she hurried to meet with the creditor and pay her bill. What a day of rejoicing that was! Not only did she have enough to pay her bill in full, but also she had plenty of leftover money for her and her two sons to live. Praise the Lord for His helping hand in her life!

The hand of God is as active now as it has ever been. One of the many things His hand does is help those who follow Him. If you have chosen to follow the Lord, ask for the Lord's hand to help you. "Let thine hand help me; for I have chosen thy precepts" (Ps. 119:173). Don't expect His hand to help you if you are not doing what is right.

When David was a shepherd boy, he protected his sheep with his hands. With his bare hands he killed a bear and a lion (1 Sam. 17:34-35). Our Good Shepherd is the Lord, and He will keep His sheep (those who believe in Him) in His hands. "For he is our God; and we are the people of his pasture, and the sheep of his hand" (Ps. 95:7).

God is a great God. He loves us, and one of the ways He demonstrates His love is by giving us a helping hand. "Shew thy marvellous lovingkindness, O thou that savest by thy right hand them which put their trust in thee from those that rise up against them" (Ps. 17:7). Put your full trust in God's hand. Because His hand is in control, with confidence you can leave your needs in His hand.

A Lesson to Learn from the Widow of a College Student

As soon as troubles came her way, the Widow of a College Student wanted to know what God wanted her to do. Then, when she found out what He wanted her to do, she did it. If you are facing troubles and truly desire to know what God wants you to do, talk to Him. Read His word (Ps. 119:24). He may encourage you to seek a godly counselor or pastor for advice—the Bible many times mentions the wisdom in seeking wise counsel. Know that God will speak to you. And when He does, make sure you listen and act.

When troubles come your way, make your way to the Lord. When you take your troubles to Him, the Lord says He will be there for you. "He shall call upon me, and I will answer him: I will be with him in trouble; I will deliver him, and honour him" (Ps. 91:15).

How did her faith affect her family?

Her faith affected her two sons. Had she not gone to Elisha in her time of need, she would not have known what to do. Also, she had faith in doing what Elisha told her, and her sons saw the miracle. Because she followed through Elisha's advice and worked hard, she paid off her debt. This kept her two sons from living a life as slaves.

Our Personal Prayer

Lord, so many times we have failed in going to You first for help with our troubles. Forgive us for forgetting about going to You first. Help us to make it a habit to take our problems to You. We truly want to hear from You and do what You say.

Questions to Consider

1. When your next problem or major decision comes your way, what should you do?_____
    _____

2. What are some ways you can help your financial situation?
    _____
    _____

3. Is there something you need to seek wise counsel about? Before talking with a counselor, what should you determine?
    _____
    _____

4. Is there a trouble you are going through that you need to leave in His hand?_____
    _____

Chapter Two

Tamar

A Woman Whose Great Sin Was Pardoned by God's Great Mercy

Genesis 38:16-30

Do you ever feel that your sins are too great to be forgiven? Or, do you ever feel that someone you label as "a great sinner" can never receive pardon for her sins? Thankfully, our feelings about the matter don't dictate God's actions. Though we may not understand the depths of His great mercy, God is a merciful God who pardons sin. "Pardon" means to release a guilty person from his offenses. We all need to be pardoned from our sins. Thankfully, God's mercy and pardon are available to **all** of us, despite whatever sins we have committed.

A maiden pleaded with Napoleon for the life of her father, a deserter, condemned to be executed. A frown gathered upon Napoleon's brow as he answered, "He has already twice deserted, and do you ask for his life?" "Sir" she answered, "I do not ask for justice but, for mercy." Her plea was granted.

Tamar deserved great punishment for something wicked she did. Yet God in His merciful kindness gave her pardon. We don't see God's hand of judgment in her life; we only see His hand of mercy.

Waiting for the Father

After Judah and his nine brothers sold their brother Joseph to a group of Ishmaelites, Judah decided it was time to move away from the family. He left his family in Hebron (Gen. 38:1) and went to Adullam to see a friend of his named Hirah. While in Adullam, a Canaanite lady caught his eye (Gen. 38:12 says her dad's name was Shuah but there is no mention of her name). Judah married her, and she gave him three sons –Er, Onan, and Shelah.

Tamar was picked by Judah to marry Er, his firstborn (Gen. 38:6). Their marriage did not last long, for her husband's wickedness made her a widow. "And Er, Judah's firstborn, was wicked in the sight of the LORD; and the LORD slew him" (Gen. 38:7). Judah knew that he must marry his second son to Tamar for Er's name to live on.

Though Moses had not given the law at this point, it was customary for the brother next in line to marry his brother's widow. "Levirate marriage (the marriage of a widow to the brother of her deceased husband) was widely practiced and later incorporated into the law of Moses...Deut. 25:5-10."[4]

Onan had no choice but to marry Tamar. He knew that if she got pregnant their child would have Er's inheritance, not his. Because Onan wanted his brother's inheritance, he decided to prevent Tamar from even getting pregnant. This made the Lord very angry. "And the thing which he did displeased the LORD: wherefore he slew him also" (Gen. 38:10).

After the sudden death of her second husband, her father-in-law told her, "Remain a widow at thy father's house, till Shelah my son be grown: for he said, Lest peradventure he die also, as his brethren did. And Tamar went and dwelt in her father's house" (Gen. 38:11). Up until now, Judah had kept his word with her, and she didn't mind waiting on her father-in-law.

Maybe Tamar didn't know Judah blamed her for Er and Onan's death, but she must have suspected his feelings. Surely, she, too, wondered why both of her husbands had unexpectedly dropped dead. While living with her parents again, she waited for Judah to marry her to Shelah. She waited and waited and waited.

When we wait for a promise from man, we may end up waiting a long time for something that may never even happen. In fact, the only thing we can depend on from man is knowing we can't depend on him. Though there will be times we will have to wait on our heavenly Father, we know we can depend on Him.

Waiting on the Lord renews our strength for our time of action. "But they that wait upon the LORD shall renew their strength; they shall mount up with wings as eagles; they shall run, and not be weary; and they shall walk, and not faint" (Is. 40:31). The word *wait* in Is. 40:31 does not mean to sit around and do nothing; it means to expect or look. "My soul, wait thou only upon God; for my expectation is from him" (Ps. 62:5).

I had to wait on the Lord in the area of finding a husband. During my waiting period, I was on the lookout for any man that qualified to fit my list of expectations (and it wasn't short either!). While on Christmas vacation in December 2003, my family and I visited Faith Baptist Church in Cottonwood, Arizona, and I met the cute single pastor. After getting to know him a little bit, I realized he was definitely husband material for me, and a year-and-a-half later (when I was 28) we married. I'm so glad I waited on the Lord. He sent me the desire of my heart. Like me, you will never regret waiting on the Lord; for He will always do what's best for you.

Not Going to the Person with Whom She Had a Problem

Tamar noticed when Shelah was a grown man (Gen. 38:14) that Judah still had not said anything about her marriage to Shelah. Frustration came over her, and she wondered what she should do. She had realized that for the name of Judah's tribe's to live on she must marry Shelah and have children. While thinking about her choices, she suddenly realized Shelah wasn't her only option. An idea—one she knew could work if planned just right—came into her head.

"In the process of time" (Gen. 38:12), she heard news that Judah's wife died. ("In the process of time" implies that many days multiplied or perhaps several years passed away.) Judah comforted himself after his wife's death, and when the mourning period was over he decided to get together with his friend Hiram.

Sheep-shearing season had come upon the land. It was about the end of March,[5] and Judah and Hiram traveled six miles to Timnath to

17

shear the sheep.[6] Because sheep-shearing was known as a time of entertainment, feasts, and parties, Judah looked forward to having some fun with his friend.

"And it was told Tamar, saying, Behold thy father in law goeth up to Timnath to shear his sheep" (Gen. 38:13). Now was the time for her to go through with her plan. She quickly dressed out of her widow's clothing, covered herself with a veil, wrapped herself, and sat in an open place on the way to Timnath. Instead of going to Judah and telling him how hurt she was, she had decided to take matters into her own hands.

We have all been hurt by someone and by her broken promises. You can't control what people do to you, but you can control how you react. Jesus said that if your brother has offended you, you must go to that person and let him know. "Moreover if thy brother shall trespass against thee, go and tell him his fault between thee and him alone: if he shall hear thee, thou hast gained thy brother" (Matt. 18:15).

Yes, it's awkward, but it's God's way. Going to someone and telling them their fault will result in gaining a "brother." Most ladies have a tendency to not tell someone they have been hurt, harbor bitter feelings toward that person, and react irrationally (like Tamar did). Have you ever known some people who could tell you every person who has wronged them? Their hearts are overgrown with bitterness, resulting in squeezing out the Holy Spirit's working in their life.

Here are some thoughts on going to the person who has offended you. First of all, pray. Pray that you will have a Christ-like love for that person (1 Jn. 4:7). Second, go to him alone (Matt. 18:15). Third, make sure you are talking to that person in the spirit of meekness (Gal. 6:1). The person may respond the right way or may not (see Matt. 18:16-17 to find out what to do if the response is negative). Remember, you are not accountable for how that person responds, but you are accountable to make sure you have done what God wants you to do.

Doing Something Wrong to Make Something Right

When Judah was walking along the road, he saw a woman dressed in harlot clothing. Not having any idea it was his daughter-in-law Tamar, he approached her. He told her he wanted to use her services. Tamar, knowing what he wanted, asked him, "What wilt thou give me?" (Gen. 38:16).

He told her he would give her a goat from his flock. And she said, "Wilt thou give me a pledge, till thou send it? And he said, What pledge shall I give thee? And she said, Thy signet, and thy bracelets, and thy staff that is in thine hand. And he gave it her, and came in unto her, and she conceived by him" (Gen. 38:17-18).

After being with Judah, she quickly returned to her father's house to take off her veil and put on her widow's clothing. She took the items Judah had given her for a pledge and made sure they were hidden in a good spot, for she didn't want anyone to discover what she had done.

Meanwhile, Judah had sent his friend Hiram with a goat to pay the harlot. Hiram looked everywhere for her but could not find her. After he told this to Judah, Judah said, "Let her take it to her, lest we be shamed: behold, I sent this kid, and thou hast not found her" (Gen. 38:23). In other words, Judah told Hiram to not ask anyone else about his stuff so that no one would find out he had been tricked by a harlot. He feared being made fun of by his friends more than he feared God's displeasure at what he had done.

Tamar maybe had the right motive behind her wicked act, but it is never right to do wrong. Have you heard the sayings, "It is never right to do wrong, or one wrong plus a right still makes a wrong"? Though simple, these sayings have been a help to me. No matter what your motive is, you should never do something wrong to make something right.

A wrong deed will bring wrong results. "But he that doeth wrong shall receive for the wrong which he hath done" (Col. 3:25). If you want something to be done right, make sure you are doing right. God's ways must be done His way, not your way.

Since we are all prone to do wrong, what should we do when we commit a wrongful act? Acknowledge your wrongdoing. Then openly talk to the Lord about your mistake. Confess your sin, and be assured that God has forgiven you (Ps. 32:5). "If we confess our sins, he is faithful and just to forgive us our sins, and to cleanse us from all unrighteousness" (1 John 1:9).

Deserving Punishment, Receiving God's Pardon

Three months later, Judah found out Tamar was pregnant. "It was told Judah, saying, Tamar thy daughter in law hath played the harlot; and also, behold, she is with child by whoredom. And Judah said, Bring her forth, and let her be burnt" (Gen. 38:24).

Judah, reacting quickly to the news, probably saw his chance to get rid of Tamar and free Shelah to marry someone else. Because Judah had told her she would one day marry Shelah, the betrothal had been arranged; she had been considered Shelah's wife. Though the law had not been brought forth yet, those who committed adultery were put to death.

When someone came by the house of Tamar's dad to get her, she gathered up Judah's items he had given her. "When she was brought forth, she sent to her father in law, saying, By the man, whose these are, am I with child: and she said, Discern, I pray thee, whose are these, the signet, and bracelets, and staff" (Gen. 38:25).

Judah shamefully admitted that "She hath been more righteous than I; because that I gave her not to Shelah my son. And he knew her again no more" (Gen. 38:26). He knew he had treated her unfairly and had not kept his promise. (Maybe sometime after this is when Shelah married and had his own family as seen in 1 Chron. 4:21.)

Perhaps because of Tamar's sin, the Lord made sure she would have a hard time during her delivery. She had carried twins; during her labor, one of her sons stuck out his hand. The midwife bound some scarlet thread around his hand and stated that he had come out first. As the baby pulled his hand back inside, the other baby seized the moment and came out first.

This first born baby's name was Pharez, meaning breach (the act of breaking; a gap). Then Pharez's brother, Zarah, made his way out with the scarlet thread around his hand (Gen. 38:28-30). Tamar was very happy to have two sons. Though she deserved great punishment for her sin (Deut. 22:23-24), instead God gave her pardon.

God, the ultimate Judge, grants pardon to those who deserve punishment. Every person on this earth deserves punishment for his sin (Rom. 6:23). Yet, Jesus Christ came to pardon us from our sin by shedding his blood on the cross. When we confess our sin and need for Jesus to be our Savior, we will receive pardon for our punishment.

John Bunyan, the famous author of Pilgrim's Progress, claimed to have been "morally reprehensible" when he was a teenager as stated in his autobiography *Grace Abounding*. Confessing to sins of profanity and dancing, he viewed himself as having unpardonable sins. After he became saved, he became a writer and a preacher. It was then he realized that no matter how great his sin was in his life, God's pardon was greater.

> Thus far did I come laden with my sin,
> Nor could aught ease the grief that I was in,
> Till I came hither. What a place is this!
> Must here be the beginning of my bliss?
> Must here the burden fall from off my back?
> Must here the strings that bound it to me crack?
> Blest cross! blest sepulchre; blest rather be
> The Man that there was put to shame for me.—*Bunyan*

A pardon can only be given to someone who accepts it. God will "abundantly pardon" (Is. 55:7) those who come to him. "And I will cleanse them from all their iniquity, whereby they have sinned against me; and I will pardon all their iniquities, whereby they have sinned, and whereby they have transgressed against me" (Jer. 33:8).

21

A Lesson to Learn from God the Father

We do not know Tamar's motives and could speculate ourselves to death on the issue. Did she do what she did to get vengeance from Judah? Did she do what she did because, though she was a Canaanite, she embraced the Israelite religion and "believed the promise made to Abraham and his seed, particularly that of the Messiah, who was to descend from the loins of Judah"?[7]

There are several lessons we can learn from Tamar's life, but I believe, instead of focusing on Tamar, we should focus on learning from God in this passage. You may wonder why God would use such a horrid story to start the line of David. This story is filled with deceit, incest, trickery, and fornication. Why would God want Jesus to come from this family tree? Because it shows His unfailing mercy, forgiveness, grace, and pardon. This story does tell about Tamar and Judah, but really the whole story points to God and who He is. Tamar deserved severe punishment for her actions, but God instead granted her mercy. Isn't that wonderful? I am so glad we serve a God whose mercy is never ending.

How did her faith affect her family?

Her faith affected her father-in-law. Though she went about it the wrong way, she did give Judah two sons and thereby preserved his family line. Her brother-in-law, Shelah, had gotten married and had sons (1 Chron. 4:21), but God had chosen Tamar and Judah's sons to start the line of Christ.

Her faith affected her sons Pharez and Zarah. God had chosen Pharez, of the house of Judah, to start the line for the Messiah to come. Interestingly enough, not only is his name mentioned in the genealogy listed in Matthew, but also his brother Zarah's name is mentioned as well (Matt. 1:3).

Our Personal Prayer

Lord, we know we don't deserve Your mercy and pardon in our lives. We cannot comprehend Your forgiveness in our lives when we fail You. Thank You for being a great God. May our gratitude for You encourage us to serve You with a pure heart.

Questions to Consider

1. Is there an area in your life you are having a hard time waiting on the Lord? What will happen when you wait on Him?

   _____

   _____

2. Is there someone you have a problem with and need to talk to? Perhaps someone has approached you and you have responded incorrectly. What should you do?

   _____

   _____

3. Based on 1 John 1:9, what is something you should be in the habit of doing daily?

   _____

   _____

4. Do you have a hard time believing God could pardon and use someone who committed such a horrible sin? What is one thing you learned about God from Tamar's life?

   _____

   _____

Chapter Three

Four Women Who Gave Their Lives to God's Work

What you are is God's gift to you; what you give back to Him is your gift to Him. You will never regret giving your life to God's work. When you honor the Lord with your life, know that He will bestow honor upon you. "Therefore, my beloved brethren, be ye stedfast, unmoveable, always abounding in the work of the Lord, forasmuch as ye know that your labour is not in vain in the Lord" (1 Cor. 15:58).

You may not see the results of your labor here on earth. You may not receive any pats on the back, either, but be assured your life is pleasing your Savior. The Bible records four ladies, none of whom could win a popularity contest among other ladies, who gave their lives to God's work. Mrs. Noah, Lydia, Mary of Jerusalem, and Priscilla each used what God had individually given her and gave all she had for the Lord's work.

Mrs. Noah: A Help Meet to Her Husband
Gen. 6-9

Mrs. Noah faced the challenge of keeping her family free from the world's wicked ways (Gen. 6:5). A mother to three sons—Shem, Ham, and Japheth—she had a huge job. When Noah came home to inform Mrs. Noah that God was going to destroy the earth in a flood, she was shocked! Noah said God would spare their families' lives along with two, and some seven, of each kind of animal in a boat called an ark.

She saw Noah's faith (Heb. 11:7) as he set to work on his task. God had given Noah specific instructions on building the ark. The frame was huge—about 450 feet long and three stories high. I'm sure Mrs.

25

Noah heard many comments from her family and neighbors about that ark and all the food her family was gathering!

While Noah was also a "preacher of righteousness" (2 Pet. 2:5) for one hundred and twenty years (Gen. 6:3), she supported him though he never saw one convert. "She stood faithfully by her preacher-husband though he was often crushed by the futility of his ministry to a world which had forgotten God. Together they faced the scorn and contempt of one hundred and twenty years of ministry to a world that stopped its ears to God's Word."[8]

Finally, the ark was finished, and the amazing day came when male and female animals, two unclean and seven clean (needed for sacrifices), fowl, and creeping things moved on the ark (it sounds simple, but what an amazing sight that must have been!). Noah and Mrs. Noah, along with their three sons and daughters-in-law, boarded their new home and waited (Gen. 7:10).

God was giving the world seven days to repent before the flood came, but on the seventh day it was still just the eight of them. After the Lord shut them in the ark (Gen. 7:16), "the fountains of the great deep broke up and it rained for forty days, destroying every living thing" (Gen. 7:23). This family went through so much together: grieving over their dead family members, taking on new veterinary skills, fighting sickness, waiting to spy land, and imagining what lay ahead in life.

After living on the ark for more than a year, Mrs. Noah, her family, and all the animals happily stepped on dry ground! The Lord was pleased when Noah built an altar and offered sacrifices to Him; He blessed them and told them to have lots of children. Mrs. Noah was relieved to hear God promise He would never flood the entire earth again and sent a rainbow as a sign of His covenant. What a good helper she had been to her Lord and her husband.

The term *help meet* goes back to Adam and Eve in the Garden of Eden. Though a perfect man in a perfect world, Adam still had needs to be met—needs of companionship, tending the garden, and having children. We were created to meet our husband's needs (1 Cor. 11:8-9).

"And the LORD God said, It is not good that the man should be alone; I will make him an help meet for him" (Gen. 2:18).

When you are helping meet your husband's needs, your desire will be to him. Know his likes and dislikes. Be aware of what brings him stress. Pray for him. Set aside your personal ambitions and focus on helping him instead. Tune out friends and family who ridicule you for being "old-fashioned." Lastly, keep your heart right before the Lord so you can be right with your husband.

"There is no loss of dignity in subordination when it serves a higher purpose. God made you to be a help meet to your husband so you can bolster him, making him more productive and efficient at whatever he chooses to do."[9] Your main job as a wife is to complete and complement your husband.

Mary of Jerusalem: A Helpful Lady Who Gave Her Resources to the Lord's Work
Acts 12:12, 15:37

A resident of Jerusalem, Mary was a wealthy lady who owned a large house. She had a brother named Barnabas, from the island of Cyprus (Acts 4:36), who later sold his land for the church to have money (Acts 4:37). Mary kept her big house in Jerusalem, for she knew it would be more of a help for the apostles than money gained from it.

Her house had a large guest chamber Jesus used. The disciples had asked Jesus where He wanted to celebrate the Passover (Mark 14:12), and Jesus wanted it at Mary's house. He sent two disciples to find "a large upper room furnished and prepared" (Mark 14:15). Mary's large upper room was ready for her Master's use. It was that upper room where Jesus and His disciples broke bread the night before His crucifixion. After Jesus ascended to heaven, it was that upper room where Jesus' followers fellowshipped and prayed (Acts 1:13-14).

When the apostle Peter was imprisoned by Herod Agrippa (Acts 12:1), prayer was "made without ceasing of the church unto God for him" (Acts 12:5). This prayer meeting was being held at Mary's house "where many were gathered together praying" (Acts 12:12). After Peter was freed by an angel and walked in the streets of Jerusalem, he knew the other disciples would be at Mary's house.

"And as Peter knocked at the door of the gate, a damsel came to hearken, named Rhoda" (Acts 12:13). "The word 'damsel' means a female slave."[10] Rhoda, like Barnabas, was from the island of Cyprus and it is believed that either Barnabas or Mary brought her to Jerusalem. Rhoda cautiously investigated the noise outside the gate, for these were scary times. Imagine her surprise when she heard Peter's voice! Though the Christians didn't believe her at first, they discovered it was Peter! No doubt Mary had a great influence in the life of Rhoda.

Mary's son John Mark (Col. 4:10) "must have been fairly familiar with the personal teaching of the apostles themselves. He may have been a direct convert of Peter because the apostle later identified him as his son (1 Pet. 5:13), a son in the faith."[11] John Mark went with Paul and Barnabas on a mission's trip and journeyed with them from Jerusalem to Antioch to Cyprus. After Cyprus, he quit and headed home to Jerusalem (Acts 13:13). Though his unfaithfulness caused contention between Paul and Barnabas, he matured in the faith and Paul later said he was profitable to him in the ministry (2 Tim. 4:11).

Mary helped by giving her house, wealth, and even her son to the Lord's work. Her trust was in her Lord Jesus and not in her riches. "Charge them that are rich in this world, that they be not highminded, nor trust in uncertain riches, but in the living God, who giveth us richly all things to enjoy; That they do good, that they be rich in good works, ready to distribute, willing to communicate" (1 Tim. 6:17-18).

The Lord has given you resources to be used for His work. You might not think they are as good as someone else's, and maybe they aren't, but they are yours. It is what you have that He wants for His work.

Whatever resources He has given you—nice possessions, talents, extra time, a listening ear, a healthy body—can be a help if given to His work. "The righteous giveth and spareth not" (Prov. 21:26). Are you willing to help your Lord's work by giving what He has given you?

Lydia: A Heart the Lord Opened
Acts 16:13-15

Originally from Thyatira, Lydia moved to Philippi and started a purple dyeing business. Thyatira, a province of Asia, "was famous in the ancient world for its purple dye."[12] Philippi was a Roman colony, meaning lots of wealthy Romans lived there; her business was probably very successful.

On the Sabbath day, Lydia left the city and spent time at a river. With other women, she would pray and worship the Lord. One Sabbath day, she met the apostles Paul, Luke, and Silas and heard them speak. "The word heard...is in the imperfect tense. This indicates she probably heard Paul more than once. The Lord had prepared her heart through the teaching and preaching of the Word of God."[13]

Through Paul's teachings (Acts 16:14), the Lord opened her heart to the truth. Even her household believed and were baptized. After her salvation, Lydia "besought us, saying, If ye have judged me to be faithful to the Lord, come into my house, and abide there. And she constrained us" (Acts 16:15). She willingly gave her house and resources for the Lord's work.

In Philippi, Paul and Silas were beaten and imprisoned. After the Lord set them free, and the Philippian jailor and family were saved and baptized, Paul and Silas headed to Lydia's house, where she was housing other Christian brethren. Lydia probably gasped when she saw the bruises on them, but that didn't deter her newfound faith and service.

Her conversion was the beginning of the church at Philippi, and this church helped Paul four times. "I thank my God upon every remembrance of you...For your fellowship in the gospel from the first day until now" (Philippians 1:3, 5). The "first day" was a reference to Lydia.

Though Paul had originally wanted to be a missionary to Asia, the Lord had closed that door (Acts 16:6). Isn't it interesting, though, that Lydia, his first convert in Macedonia (Europe), was originally from

Asia? Lydia's conversion all started from a heart God opened. Paul did the talking, but the Holy Spirit did the working.

It is the Holy Spirit who works in one's heart, but it is our job to prepare one's heart. You cannot force anyone to accept Jesus to be her Savior, but you can start preparing her heart to respond to the Holy Spirit. Don't give up on her; instead, give her to the Lord and see Him work.

Paul said, "I have planted, Apollos watered; but God gave the increase. So then neither is he that planteth any thing, neither he that watereth; but God that giveth the increase. Now he that planteth and he that watereth are one: and every man shall receive his own reward according to his own labour. For we are labourers together with God" (I Cor. 3:6-9). You're not working alone for God's work, but working with Him for His work.

Have you ever spent time explaining God's plan of salvation to someone, but only saw her reject Christ? It's discouraging! But wait…you did what God wanted you to do; you helped prepare the soil of her heart for the Holy Spirit. You planted a seed, and you may never know until eternity what may become of it.

Priscilla: A Helper of Her Church Family
Acts 18:1-2

Priscilla lived in the city of Rome with her husband, Aquila, until Emperor Claudius decided to banish the Jews from Italy. "An early church tradition states they were driven out over rioting caused by a certain 'Chrestus'."[14] This "Chrestus" is possibly a reference to Jesus Christ. Because Aquila was Jewish (it is uncertain whether Priscilla was a Jew or Gentile), this couple was banished from Rome.

Priscilla and Aquila moved to the city of Corinth, where they set up their tent-making business. Corinth was a port city located in southern Greece and was known for its wealth and worldliness. In Corinth, they met a missionary named Paul who also was a tentmaker. Because he needed a place to stay, they let him lodge with them and quickly became friends. Some believe he led them to Christ, but if so, there is no mention of their being his first converts in Corinth. It is more likely they had already been Christians before they knew Paul.

When Paul left Corinth, Priscilla and Aquila went with him to Ephesus (Acts 18:18). There in a synagogue they heard an eloquent preacher named Apollos speak boldly about the baptism of John. "When Aquila and Priscilla had heard, they took him unto them, and expounded unto him the way of God more perfectly" (Acts 18:26). While in Ephesus, Priscilla and Aquila helped Paul, Apollos, and Timothy start a church. Priscilla willingly agreed for the church to meet in her and Aquila's home (1 Cor. 6:19).

After Emperor Claudius died is probably when Priscilla and her husband decided to move from Ephesus to Rome.[15] Guess what they did in Rome? They opened up their home for another church to meet! What a loyal, helpful couple. Paul wrote them a greeting when he wrote a letter to the church at Rome. "Greet Priscilla and Aquila my helpers in Christ Jesus: Who have for my life laid down their own necks: unto whom not only I give thanks, but also all the churches of the Gentiles. Likewise greet the church that is in their house" (Rom. 16:3-5).

Priscilla was acknowledged for doing several things, along with her husband. First, she was commended as a helper for Jesus and sacrificing her life for Paul. Second, she received thanks from other churches for her service to the Lord's work.

Rome during this time (A.D. 54-68) was not a safe place for any Christian to be, for Nero was the emperor. He hated Christians and enjoyed persecuting and imprisoning them. When Paul was imprisoned in Rome under Nero's reign, Priscilla and Aquila weren't there; they were back helping the church in Ephesus. When Paul wrote Second Timothy, his last book in prison before his execution, he asked Timothy to "salute Prisca [Priscilla] and Aquila" (2 Tim. 4:19).

Obviously this couple was dear to him; their helpfulness had been such a blessing to him. Paul called them his helpers (Rom. 16:3).

By looking at Priscilla's life, here are some ways you too can be a help to your church family:

- Hospitality – Are you making an effort to be hospitable to others? (Rom. 12:13)
- Friendship – Is there someone you know you need to befriend? (Prov. 18:24)
- Knowledge of the Word of God – Are you involved with studying the scriptures so that you can know how to instruct someone in right doctrine or answer her questions? (Col. 4:6)
- Fellowship – Do you desire to know others in your church and help their needs? (2 Cor. 8:4)
- Sacrificial Love – Are you willing to lay down your life for another brother or for the cause of Christ? (John 15:13)
- Unselfishness – Are you too attached to your possessions to give them up for God's will in your life? (Matt. 6:24)
- Teamwork – How far are you willing to go for the cause of Christ? (Phil. 1:27)
- Loyalty – Are you loyal to your pastor and pastor's wife? Do you do whatever you can to help ease their burdens? (Heb. 6:10)

The Lord will remember all the help you give to your church family. "For God is not unrighteous to forget your work and labour of love, which ye have shewed toward his name, in that ye have ministered to the saints, and do minister" (Heb. 6:10).

A Lesson to Learn from These Four Ladies

None of these four ladies regrets that she gave her life to God's work. If your life were to end tomorrow, would you regret you didn't give your life to His work or would you rejoice you did all you could do for Him? Robert Frost once said, "The world is full of willing people; some willing to work—the rest willing to let them. Which kind of person are you?" Are you willing to give your life to God's work or not? You only have one life. Are you using it for your Lord and for His work?

How did their faith affect their family?

Mrs. Noah's faith affected her husband and sons. "When God destroyed this world, her boys were the only boys worth saving (the sons of a preacher!)."[16]

Mary's faith affected her son Mark. She had served her Lord and saw her son serve the Lord. John Mark wrote the book of Mark. He also, according to tradition, started a church in Alexandria after Barnabas' death and was martyred around A.D. 62.

Lydia's faith affected her whole household. They "were saved and baptized. No doubt her faith emboldened others."[17]

Priscilla's faith affected her husband Aquila. They are mentioned side-by-side in the Bible as serving together, housing churches, and helping Paul.

Our Personal Prayer

Thank You Lord for giving us life. We desire for our life to help others and You. May our life please You as we use it for Your work.

Questions to Consider

1. How can your loyalty to your husband, friends, and family affect them?

   _____

   _____

2. What resources or talents do you have that you should give to God's work?

   _____

   _____

3. How can you be a servant to others and to your Lord Jesus?

_____

_____

4. According to James 4:14, why is it important we work hard today for the Lord?

_____

_____

Chapter Four

Jezebel

A Prideful Woman Who Wanted Power

1 Kings 16:29-33

Do you know that if you are a Christian you have access to unlimited power? This power comes from the Holy Spirit, who is a gift from God, given to you on the day of your salvation. "But as many as received him, to them gave he power to become the sons of God, even to them that believe on his name" (John 1:12). Not only are we given power over death (Ps. 49:15), but also power to help us in life (Is. 40:29). This power is meant to point people to Christ—not to use for ourselves.

Believing himself to be as powerful as God, Satan's heart was filled with pride, causing his fall from heaven (Is. 14:12). Like her father the devil, Jezebel was a prideful woman who wanted power for her own selfish desires.

Clinging to Her Heathen Roots

Jezebel's roots came from a country called Zidon. "The inhabitants of Zidon were among the nations of Canaan…they oppressed the Israelites on their first entrance into the country (Judg. 10:12), and appear to have lived a luxurious, reckless life (Judg. 18:7)."[18] The Zidonians worshipped Ashtoreth (1 Kings 11:5), Baal (1 Kings 16:31), and many other gods (Judges 10:6).

A princess of Zidon, Jezebel surely grew up a very spoiled child. Her father, Ethbaal, was the king. (Notice her father's name has "Baal" in it. Baal was the name of the sun god.[19]) Because idolatry was such a huge influence in Jezebel's home, she would always remain faithful to her gods.

When she married Ahab, the king of Israel, her idolatrous ways soon influenced him. Ahab "took to wife Jezebel the daughter of Ethbaal king of the Zidonians, and went and served Baal, and worshipped him. And he reared up an altar for Baal in the house of Baal, which he had built in Samaria. And Ahab made a grove; and Ahab did more to provoke the LORD God of Israel to anger than all the kings of Israel that were before him" (1 Kings 16:31-33).

Maybe you don't think your roots are as heathen as Jezebel's were, but you are wrong. Until you have Christ in your heart, your roots go back to serving the devil. Every one of our lives has at some point belonged to the devil (Gal. 4:3-6). It is when we ask Christ into our heart that we have a new life and a new Master.

Your new life can no longer mix in with your old roots. You must choose to separate from your old ways. You can't keep one arm in the world, touching things that are in your past, and one arm clinging to Jesus. Jesus wants you to be separated from the world so that He can have communion with you.

"And what agreement hath the temple of God with idols? for ye are the temple of the living God; as God hath said, I will dwell in them, and walk in them; and I will be their God, and they shall be my people. Wherefore come out from among them, and be ye separate, saith the Lord, and *touch not the unclean thing* (italics mine); and I will receive you" (2 Cor. 6:16-17).

When you let go of the world you will be able to cling to Jesus.

Wanting God's Work to Be Destroyed

When Israel followed Jezebel in her idolatrous ways, the whole nation suffered. The Lord decided to punish Israel by sending a drought, meaning there would be no rain or even dew. When Jezebel heard the prophet Elijah informing King Ahab the Lord would send no rain for years (1 Kings 17:1), she was infuriated! Oh, how she hated Elijah and his God! I'm sure she faithfully worshipped her idols, desperately trying to bring rain to the land and prove Elijah wrong. The sight of everything shriveling up from no water must have made her so angry.

Because she hated not having things under her control, she decided to "cut off the prophets of the LORD" (1 Kings 18:4). Her hatred for God gave her strength from the devil to kill many prophets. During this sad time, God sent a man named Obadiah to hide one hundred of His prophets in two caves and to feed them.

Though a drought was taking place, Jezebel personally fed at her own table 450 prophets of Baal and 400 prophets of the grove. It was these prophets who were invited by Elijah to attend a contest on Mount Carmel. Jezebel decided to stay home, but King Ahab "sent unto all the children of Israel, and gathered the prophets together unto mount Carmel" (1 Kings 18:20).

Elijah issued a challenge to all that gathered from Israel. "How long halt ye between two opinions? if the LORD be God, follow him: but if Baal, then follow him" (1 Kings 18:21). He announced the rules of the contest: "Let them [false prophets] therefore give us two bullocks; and let them choose one bullock for themselves, and cut it in pieces, and lay it on wood, and put no fire under: and I will dress the other bullock, and lay it on wood, and put no fire under: And call ye on the name of your gods, and I will call on the name of the LORD: and the God that answereth by fire, let him be God" (1 Kings 18:23-24).

After the false prophets called on Baal all day and still received no fire, Elijah then called the people to watch him repair a broken down altar for the Lord. Using twelve stones, he constructed an altar, dug a trench, added wood, and arranged the pieces of the bull on top. Next, he ordered twelve barrels of water to be poured on top.

Elijah prayed to God, asking Him to hear his prayer and turn the people's hearts back to God. "Then the fire of the LORD fell, and consumed the burnt sacrifice" (1 Kings 18:38). The people were amazed and believed! Elijah killed the false prophets and then prayed for rain. As King Ahab headed back home to Jezreel, Elijah even outran his chariot of fine horses. What power God gave to Elijah!

Jezebel was outraged when she heard what happened! She immediately called for a messenger to tell Elijah she would kill him (1 Kings 19:2). Having already killed hundreds of God's prophets, she was very capable of killing Elijah, as well. She hated Elijah and wanted God's work to be destroyed.

I believe Jezebel worked harder at destroying the work of God than many of us strive to keep His work alive. Why are many ungodly people willing to use all of their time, money, and resources to destroy God's work while we as Christians are so apathetic about doing anything for Him?

When Jesus stood before Pilate, He was alone. "But the chief priests and elders persuaded the multitude that they should ask Barabbas, and destroy Jesus" (Matt. 27:20). The chief priests and elders knew that in order for Jesus to be destroyed, the multitude of people needed to do nothing on Jesus' behalf. Though the multitude of people weren't the ringleaders or even important people, by speaking up they could have prevented Jesus from going to the cross. Instead, they chose to do nothing for Him.

If you are not striving to keep God's work alive, you are letting His work be destroyed. Don't think the only people who destroy God's work are people who hate Him; it can be anyone who's not doing anything for Him. Are you doing nothing or something for Christ?

Using the King's Name

One day Jezebel went to see Ahab and found him in his bedroom pouting. He informed her that an Israelite named Naboth would not sell his vineyard to Ahab because it went against God's command. Jezebel quickly reminded him that as king of Israel he should be able to have anything he wanted.

After comforting him by telling him she would get the vineyard for him (I Kings 21:5-7), she wrote letters in Ahab's name and sealed them with his seal. These were sent to certain nobles (notice, not noble men) in the city. "And she wrote in the letters, saying, Proclaim a fast,

38

and set Naboth on high among the people: And set two men, sons of Belial, before him, to bear witness against him, saying, Thou didst blaspheme God and the king. And then carry him out, and stone him, that he may die" (1 Kings 21:9-10).

The men of Belial quickly carried out her orders and killed Naboth. (Note: Because of 2 Kings 9:26, I also believe they killed Naboth's sons so they couldn't inherit their dad's vineyard). With Naboth and his family now dead, Jezebel commanded Ahab to claim Naboth's vineyard. "Arise, take possession of the vineyard of Naboth the Jezreelite, which he refused to give thee for money: for Naboth is not alive, but dead" (1 Kings 21:15). Ahab hurried to take possession of his new vineyard, but his joy was short lived when he saw the prophet Elijah.

The Lord had sent Elijah to prophesy judgment on Ahab, his family, and Jezebel. "Behold, I [God] will bring evil upon thee, and will take away thy posterity, and will cut off from Ahab him that pisseth against the wall...And of Jezebel also spake the LORD, saying, The dogs shall eat Jezebel by the wall of Jezreel" (1 Kings 21:21, 23).

Though Ahab humbled himself before the Lord when he heard Elijah's prophecy, he returned to ignoring the Lord. Rejecting the counsel of a prophet of the Lord (1 Kings 22:14-23), he and Jehoshophat, the king of Judah, went to wage war against the Syrians. During this conflict, Ahab was killed by an arrow someone randomly shot (1 Kings 22:34). The punishment for Ahab and his family was beginning because Jezebel had used the power of her king's name to sign the letters.

As Christians, our King has given us the privilege of using His name. Since we represent our King, everything we do should be done in His name. "And whatsoever ye do in word or deed, do all in the name our Lord Jesus" (Col. 3:17). And every word or act we do should bring glory to His name. "That the name of our Lord Jesus Christ may be glorified in you, and ye in him" (2 Thess. 1:12).

The name Christian came at the time the disciples had a church in Antioch (Acts 11:26) around A.D. 43.[20] It was a name given to those who identified with following Jesus Christ. The disciples didn't start the

39

term, but used other words such as brethren or saints to distinguish them. King Agrippa referred to Paul as a Christian (Acts 26:28) because he knew Paul's actions backed up his beliefs.

Since the name Christian in today's society can mean any number of beliefs, tell people you are a "born again Christian." This will identify you not only as a follower of Christ but also a saved individual. If you are saved, you have a responsibility to your King to use His name and do great things for Him through His name.

Hindering Her Children from Doing Right

Not only was the wicked murderess Jezebel a wife, she was also a mother (and perhaps a grandmother at this time). She had a daughter named Athaliah and two sons named Ahaziah and Jehoram.

Athaliah married Jehoram, the king of Judah (Jehoram's dad was Jehoshophat). "And he [Jehoram] walked in the way of the kings of Israel, as did the house of Ahab: *for the daughter of Ahab was his wife* (italics mine): and he did evil in the sight of the LORD" (2 Kings 8:18). Now both Israelite kingdoms, Israel and Judah, were exposed to idolatry and Jezebel's influence. Her life would soon end from punishment from the Lord (see chapter five for more details of her life).

Ahaziah took the throne after Ahab was killed. "And he did evil in the sight of the Lord, and walked in the way of his father, and in the way of *his mother* (italics mine)...for he served Baal" (1 Kings 22:52-53). When great sickness came upon him (2 Kings 1:2-4), Elijah the prophet told him he would die because he had turned to his idols instead of to the Lord for healing.

Jehoram, also known as Joram, was Jezebel's other son. (Note: this is not the same Jehoram whom Athaliah married.) "He wrought evil in the sight of the LORD" and cleaved unto the sins of a man named Jeroboam (2 Kings 3:2-3). Because God ordered a man named Jehu to "smite the house of Ahab" (2 Kings 9:7), Jehoram was soon killed. Jehu ordered his captain to cast the dead body into the field of Naboth's vineyard.

At home in Jezreel, Jezebel looked out a window and saw Jehu's chariot enter the gates. He said, "Who is on my side? who?" (2 Kings 9:32). Some eunuchs standing by looked at Jehu, and he told them to throw Jezebel out her window (I'm sure she put up a fight!). After being killed by the fall, some dogs feasted on her dead body. Her life filled with wickedness finally came to an end, but, unfortunately, hindered many others from doing right.

Jesus made it very clear that our life should not offend or cause others to stumble. "But whoso shall offend one of these little ones which believe in me, it were better for him that a millstone were hanged about his neck, and that he were drowned in the depth of the sea" (Matt. 18:6).

The opposite of hindering a life would be helping a life. Help by teaching children about God the Creator, salvation through Jesus, and power from the Holy Spirit (Matt. 28:19-20). If you don't have children, you can still teach and influence another child to know the Lord.

Pastor Wayne Hardy said, "I don't just want good kids. I want godly kids. I don't just want them to know a lot about God. I want them to know God."[21] This should be a goal for every mother and grandmother to have for her children and grandchildren. The best way to help others is to help them know the Lord.

A Lesson to Learn from Jezebel

Jezebel's life was empowered by the devil; but, obviously, her power and life didn't last very long. The devil may have power, but one thing we can learn from her life is that God's power prevails. It is His power that we need to seek. It is His power from which we must depend. And remember, this power is to be used for Him and for His work.

When we forget God is our source of power, we become prideful and fall (Prov. 16:18). Those who seek to be powerful for themselves will be made weak, and those who depend on power from God for His work will be made strong.

How did her faith affect her family?

Her faith affected her husband Ahab. "But there was none like unto Ahab, which did sell himself to work wickedness in the sight of the LORD, *whom Jezebel his wife stirred up* (italics mine)" (1 Kings 21:25). Her idolatry influenced her husband to do wrong, ultimately costing him his life.

Her faith affected her own children Athaliah, Ahaziah, and Jehoram. Their lives were consumed with idolatry, wickedness, and selfishness, resulting in destruction.

Her faith affected her husband's house. As a result of God sending Jehu to destroy Ahab's house, seventy of Ahab's sons were killed (2 Kings 10). Even those who weren't related to Ahab but associated with him, Jehu left "none remaining" (2 Kings 10:11, 14).

Our Personal Prayer

Lord, we admit we are helpless without You. We need You and Your power in our lives. May we try not to do things in our own strength for You. Help us not to forget that You are our source of power.

Questions to Consider

1. What are some ways you can help the work of God move forward?

   _____

   _____

2. What does God promise in Isaiah 40:29 for those who are feeling weak?

   _____

   _____

3. Is there something in the world to which you are clinging and need to let go?

   _____

   _____

4. According to Luke 10:19 and Acts 1:8, what are some reasons you need God's power in your life? How are you going to use yours?

   _____

   _____

Chapter Five

Athaliah

A Woman Who Wanted to Rule Her Own Life

2 Kings 11:1-21

If you were asked the question "Who is ruling your life?," what would be your answer? Could you with confidence say it is the Lord, or would you regretfully admit it is yourself? Would you sheepishly admit that sometimes it is you and sometimes the Lord?

When someone has complete rule in your life, you are following his rules. You are doing everything you can to please that person. Your goals, checking account, weekly events, and daily routines will indicate who is completely ruling your life. If everything you do revolves around you and your comforts, you need to honestly evaluate who you are allowing to rule your life.

You may not know who is completely ruling your life, but the devil knows. He knows to whom your heart is fully dedicated. Athaliah's life revolved around herself only, which ultimately pleased the devil. Because the devil knew Athaliah ruled her own life, he handpicked her to carry out his diabolical plan to prevent Jesus Christ's coming to earth.

An Influence for Her Kingdom

Can you imagine what life must have been like for the only daughter mentioned of Jezebel and Ahab? Her childhood probably could be summed up by the term "spoiled brat." It is highly likely she eye witnessed the great prophet Elijah's work and heard of his miracles for the Lord. However, it was idol worship like her parents practiced that caught her eye.

Her dad, King Ahab, was king of the Northern Kingdom, called Israel. He also was friends with Jehoshaphat, king of the Southern Kingdom, called Judah. Jehoshaphat, a king who "did right in the sight of the LORD" (2 Chron. 20:32), made a mistake by agreeing to the marriage of his son Jehoram to Athaliah. This marriage joined Ahab and Jezebel's influence into both of the Israelite kingdoms. Athaliah's presence in the kingdom of Judah was not a good thing—her influence would cause the kingdom to worship her idols.

Before Athaliah's father-in-law passed away, he gave Jehoram's six brothers plenty of silver, gold, and cities. Because Jehoram was his firstborn son, Jehoshaphat gave him the kingdom for when he died. Jehoram, at the age of thirty two, took over the kingdom of Judah. By this time he had married Athaliah.

After Jehoram had established himself in his kingdom, the first step he took was to murder his brothers. "Now when Jehoram was risen up to the kingdom of his father, he strengthened himself, and slew all his brethren with the sword" (2 Chron. 21:1-4). "And he walked in the way of the kings of Israel, like as did the house of Ahab: *for he had the daughter of Ahab to wife* [italics mine]: and he wrought that which was evil in the eyes of the LORD" (2 Chron. 21:6). No doubt Athaliah had encouraged him to kill his brothers, sealing his right to the throne.

Another step he took was to introduce idol worship to his kingdom. "Moreover he made high places in the mountains of Judah, and caused the inhabitants of Jerusalem to commit fornication, and compelled Judah thereto" (2 Chron. 21:11). Again, this is evidence of Athaliah's influence in the kingdom of Judah.

Right now you belong to a kingdom—either God's kingdom or the devil's kingdom. You may not be able to visibly see these kingdoms. The moment you ask Christ into your heart, your name is added to the membership list in His kingdom.

One way to help other members of God's kingdom is to influence others to do right. Your life can really encourage them to go forward for the Lord. You may not realize how other Christians, especially brand new ones, watch to see if you go soul winning, show up for special services, volunteer to help in a ministry, and just walk your talk. "That ye would walk worthy of God, who hath called you unto his kingdom and glory" (1 Thess. 2:12).

Another mission we must have for our kingdom is to see other people added to God's kingdom. This was Jesus' mission when He was here on earth, and it should be ours while we are here on earth. "And Jesus went about all the cities and villages, teaching in their synagogues, and preaching the gospel of the kingdom" (Matt. 9:35). To accomplish this, we need to be more like Jesus and less like ourselves to further His kingdom.

A Promise by God

Jehoram, Athaliah's husband, was of the house of David. Though Jehoram was a wicked man, God would not totally destroy the house of David because of a promise (2 Sam. 7:16). God instructed the prophet Elijah (who ministered in the Northern Kingdom) to send a message to Jehoram (who lived in the Southern Kingdom). Elijah informed Jehoram that he and his family would receive punishment for their wicked ways. "Behold, with a great plague will the LORD smite thy people, and thy children, and thy wives, and all thy goods: And thou shalt have great sickness by disease of thy bowels, until thy bowels fall out by reason of the sickness day by day" (2 Chron. 21:14-15).

Right after this more judgment came. The Philistines and the Arabians, who were stirred up by God, came to Judah and took away all the stuff in Jehoram's house, plus wives (too bad they didn't take Athaliah!) and sons. Yet, because God had to keep His promise to David, He had them leave them one son (2 Chron. 21:16).

Directly after this, you guessed it, more tragedy came. The Lord smote Jehoram's bowels, and he died two years later. His reign only lasted for eight years, and he "departed without being desired" (2 Chron. 21:20), meaning nobody even missed him.

Ahaziah (he also went by two other names—Azariah and Jehoahaz), was the only son left of Athaliah and Jehoram. He became the

47

king of Judah when his father died. Unfortunately, his mother's influence was his downfall. "He also walked in the ways of the house of Ahab: *for his mother was his counseller to do wickedly* (italics mine). Wherefore he did evil in the sight of the LORD like the house of Ahab: for they were his counsellers after the death of his father to his destruction" (2 Chron. 22:3-4).

Even long before the kidnapping of his brothers by the Philistines and Arabians, Ahaziah and his brothers committed a heinous crime—destroying the house of the Lord. "For the sons of Athaliah, that wicked woman, had broken up the house of God; and also all the dedicated things of the house of the LORD did they bestow upon Baalim" (2 Chron. 24:7).

Though this family was wicked, God would not totally destroy them because He had promised David that the Messiah would come from his house. God always keeps every promise He makes. "For the word of the LORD is right; and all his works are done in truth" (Ps. 33:4). Though you won't be able to count on a promise made to you by man, a promise by God can always be counted on.

If you really want to know some of God's promises, read your Bible and find them. Highlight or underline them with a colored pencil or pen. Look to His Word to find out His words. "God's promises must drive us to his precepts as our rule, and then his precepts must send us back to his promises for strength, for without his grace we can do nothing" (Matthew Henry).

Some great promises of God to claim: Phil. 4:6-7, Prov. 22:6, Ps. 37:4, Ps. 27:14, Is. 44:3, Rom. 8:38-39, Ps. 37:39, Is. 40:10-11, 29-31, and Acts 1:8. I challenge you to pick, study, meditate, pray, and memorize one. D.L. Moody said, "God never made a promise that was too good to be true."

An Instrument of Satan

Though Ahaziah's name means "upheld by Jehovah," God had never been real to Athaliah's son. His idolatrous ways were known by the Lord, who wanted Ahaziah's rule to come to an end. God sent Jehu to destroy Ahaziah. "And the destruction of Ahaziah was of God" (2 Chron. 22:7).

When Athaliah saw that her son was killed, "she arose and destroyed all the seed royal" (2 Kings 11:1). Killing her own family to gain the throne was evidence of the influence in her life of the murderess Jezebel, her mother. By desiring to rule her own life, it was apparent the devil had taken over Athaliah's life.

One thing Athaliah did not know, however, is that one of her grandsons escaped her massacre. She had not killed Joash, Ahaziah's son, either because she miscounted or didn't know her own family that well. A lady named Jehosheba, sister to Ahaziah, took and hid one-year-old Joash, with his nurse, in a bedchamber (a room believed to store bed mattresses) (2 Kings 11:2). Next, Jehosheba fled to the house of the Lord and hid Joash with the priest Jehoiada.

For six more years, Athaliah reigned over the kingdom of Judah while Joash continued hiding in the house of the Lord. Athaliah must have thought she was triumphant over destroying the house of David, but she was wrong. The devil had used her life to be instrumental in his plan of destroying the line of Judah and Jesus Christ's entry into the world, but his plan failed and God's will prevailed.

Athaliah had yielded her life as an instrument of unrighteousness, giving the devil control of her life. "Neither yield ye your members as instruments of unrighteousness unto sin: but yield yourselves unto God, as those that are alive from the dead, and your members as instruments of righteousness unto God" (Rom. 6:13). You have the choice to whom you yield your life as an instrument. May you choose to yield your instrument to God.

The word instrument has the idea of a tool. Yield your life as a tool of righteousness for God to use. He wants to use a clean tool—not a dirty one. Imagine trying to brush your teeth with a muddy toothbrush. As long as it is dirty, it won't be a very effective tool in cleaning your teeth.

How can you keep your instrument clean? Some suggestions would be the following: daily confess your sins, listen to godly music, memorize Bible verses, read your Bible, pray, tell people about Jesus, and think pure thoughts. Your life will be a more effective instrument of righteousness for the Lord if you are clean.

A People Excited about a King's Return

Unknown to Athaliah, plans were being made by Jehoiada, the priest. Having taken care of Joash, he knew the time was coming to reveal him as king. Jehoiada decided when Joash was seven years old that he would reveal his secret (2 Chron. 23:1).

Jehoiada had the captains of hundreds, Levites, and chief fathers meet him in Jerusalem. He said unto them, "Behold, the king's son shall reign, as the LORD hath said of the sons of David" (2 Chron. 23:3). He issued the orders, divided up the group, and armed them with shields and spears that had belonged to King David. Next, he brought out Joash and, along with his sons, anointed him king.

Athaliah had no clue as to what was happening. After hearing a commotion coming from the temple, she wandered over to see what was causing all the noise. Trumpets and other instruments were blaring and people were shouting. As she edged her way closer, perhaps she could hear the words "God save the king!" Enraged, she peeked into the temple and saw this scene. People were rejoicing and a little boy, standing by a pillar, wore a crown on his head.

Tearing her clothes, she shouted, "Treason, treason!" (2 Chron. 23:13). Though she tried to get away, she was captured by the captains of the guard. "So they laid hands on her; and when she was come to the entering of the horse gate by the king's house, they slew her there" (2 Chron. 23:15). (An interesting note is that horses were her father's pride and joy, and it was also horses that trampled her mother to death. Now, by the horse gate she is murdered.)

After Athaliah's death, the people, the king, and Jehoiada made a covenant to be the Lord's people only. Then they headed to the house of

Baal to destroy it and the priests of Baal. Everyone rejoiced in Athaliah's destruction and return of the king.

There is a great day coming for all Christians. It is called the Rapture. On this exciting day the Lord Jesus will come and take us Christians away. "For the Lord himself shall descend from heaven with a shout, with the voice of the archangel, and with the trump of God: and the dead in Christ shall rise first: Then we which are alive and remain shall be caught up together with them in the clouds, to meet the Lord in the air: and so shall we ever be with the Lord" (1 Thess. 4:16-17).

When I was fifteen, it seemed like all my church really talked about was the Rapture. Instead of feeling excited about it, though, I wasn't. I wanted Jesus to come later in my life. I wanted Him to come after I got my driver's license, fell in love, got married, had kids...and the list went on. Why would I feel this way, knowing that a driver's license would never compare to the wonders of heaven? It is because I was selfish. Don't let your selfish desires take away excitement you should have for Jesus' appearing.

Are you excited about the Lord's coming? If so, did you know you will receive a crown of righteousness at His appearing? "Henceforth there is laid up for me a crown of righteousness, which the Lord, the righteous judge, shall give me at that day: and not to me only, but unto all them also that love his appearing" (2 Tim. 4:8).

The Rapture of Christians will truly be an exciting day, for that's the day we will see our King. I pray that you are saved, doing God's will, and eagerly looking for the King's return.

A Lesson to Learn from Athaliah

Ruling one's own life will bring temporary pleasure but damaging long-term results. Our sinful, fleshly nature naturally wants us to have our every desire and comfort. However, by doing whatever feels good, you are letting the devil rule your life. For God to have 100% rule in your life, you will have to deny some earthly pleasures from yourself.

51

"Then said Jesus unto his disciples, If any man will come after me, let him deny himself, and take up his cross, and follow me" (Matt. 16:24).

Ultimately, the Lord will one day have total rule over everyone's life. After He comes back to earth, after the tribulation period, His throne will be established. When you die and live in Heaven, He will have full reign over your life. If you trust Him to rule your life in Heaven, why not let Him rule your life now?

How did her faith affect her family?

Athaliah's faith affected her husband Jehoram. Her wicked influence was seen when he murdered his brothers and brought idolatry into the land of Judah.

Her faith affected her sons. She was Ahaziah's counselor to do wickedly, and his wicked ways brought him destruction from the Lord. Her other sons destroyed the house of God, took the dedicated things to God, and gave them to their god, Baalim.

Her faith affected her grandchildren. Because she wanted to rule her own life and be number one, she murdered her whole family. Countless people were killed because of her wickedness.

Our Personal Prayer

Lord, may You fully rule our lives as we strive to further Your kingdom. Thank You for always keeping Your promises, and we especially look forward to the day we meet You and dwell in Your kingdom forever.

Questions to Consider

1. How are you influencing people for the kingdom of God?

   _____

   _____

2. Is there an area in your life you don't want to give your King complete reign over? What are some steps you should take?

   _____

   _____

3. What are some things you need to do to keep your life a clean instrument for God?

   _____

   _____

4. Are you excited about the Lord's return? Is there something you need to do in your life to prepare for His return?

   _____

   _____

Chapter Six

Hannah

A Woman Who Prayed and Praised with Passion
1 Samuel 1-2

What you are passionate about, you will do. What you are not passionate about you may do, but lacking passion. Are you passionate about having an incredible prayer life? If so, your passion will drive you to pray with feeling and "without ceasing" (1 Thess. 5:17). Jesus led the ultimate example in a passionate prayer life. While some of His prayers were simple, one prayer He "prayed more earnestly" (Luke 22:44). Either way, all His prayers were filled with passion.

Are you passionate about praising the Lord? As He is worthy of our prayers, He is worthy to be praised with our whole heart. "I will praise thee, O Lord my God, with all my heart" (Ps. 86:12). The writer of Psalm 119:164 stated that he praised the Lord seven times a day. Seven times! How are you doing in your praise life?

"What we win with prayer we must wear with praise."[22] May we have a passionate prayer life and praise life for our Lord. Hannah is well known for her passionate prayer in the tabernacle, but she also praised the Lord with a beautiful song of praise in 1 Samuel 2:1-11.

Facing Oppression from an Enemy

Hannah married Elkanah, who was a Levite and of the house of the Kohathites. The Kohathites were an honorable house from the tribe of Levi and known for when they carried the holy things of the tabernacle. Hannah and Elkanah lived in Ramathaim-zophim (known as Ramah in 1 Sam. 1:19), "a town located approximately two hours northwest of Jerusalem."[23]

Hannah was a lady who bore several burdens. Her husband, Elkanah, had another wife named Peninnah, who had several sons and daughters. Hannah was childless, for "the LORD had shut up her womb" (1 Sam. 1:5). When Elkanah would go to the tabernacle in Shiloh every year to worship and bring sacrifices to the Lord, he would give Peninnah and her children leftover portions of his meat. "But unto Hannah he gave a worthy portion; for he loved Hannah: but the LORD had shut up her womb" (1 Sam. 1:5).

Peninnah noticed Hannah was Elkanah's favorite wife; and, because of this, she did everything to make Hannah miserable. Whenever the two ladies would be together, Peninnah always got on Hannah's nerves. Peninnah, called Hannah's adversary, "provoked her sore" and made her fret (1 Sam. 1:6). Hannah was weary of the oppression from her enemy.

If you are a Christian, you have an enemy—the devil. Your enemy is real, and he is going to do everything he can to oppress you. To oppress means to overpower, overburden, sit or lie heavy on. What would happen if you let someone sit on you all day long? Would you put up with it? No, you would do everything you could to get that person off you. The same applies spiritually. When you feel the devil "sitting on you," with God's help get up! Don't let the devil keep you down, and don't give up. Remember, your God is bigger and His pinkie finger can throw your enemy off you!

When the devil comes to you, **seek** the refuge of your powerful, almighty God. "The LORD also will be a refuge for the oppressed, a refuge in times of trouble" (Ps. 9:9). "The eternal God is thy refuge, and underneath are the everlasting arms: and he shall thrust out the enemy from before thee" (Deut. 33:27). **Cry** out to the Lord for help. "Attend unto me, and hear me: I mourn in my complaint, and make a noise; Because of the voice of the enemy, because of the oppression of the wicked" (Ps. 55:2-3). Fully **place** your life under God's power, and you will be able to watch the devil run away from you. "Submit yourselves therefore to God. Resist the devil, and he will flee from you" (James 4:7).

You are God's possession; with His life He has bought you from the devil (Ps. 107:2). God knows the devil wants to destroy you. Can we prevail against such a powerful enemy? Yes, but only through the power of God.

Bringing Her Bitter Spirit to the Lord

Hannah's adversary provoked her "year by year." Instead of the yearly trip to the tabernacle being a time of worship and joy for Hannah, it was a time of grief. Peninnah seized that time to belittle Hannah's barren state. Hannah didn't let Peninnah's words stop her faithfulness at attending the tabernacle. However, she did let Peninnah rob her of her joy, for "she wept, and did not eat" (1 Sam. 1:7).

Hannah's cries reached Elkanah's ear. He asked her, "Why weepest thou? and why eatest thou not? and why is thy heart grieved? am not I better to thee than ten sons?" He really couldn't understand why she was sad since she had him. His words must have comforted her, for we read that, "Hannah rose up after they had eaten in Shiloh, and after they had drunk" (1 Sam. 1:9). The phrase "Hannah rose up," does not mean that she got up early; it means she rose up with strength to accomplish and endure.

With her renewed spirit, she headed to the tabernacle. When she approached, she noticed Eli was sitting on a seat by a post. Not only was Eli the high priest, but he was also a judge of Israel. She probably also saw Eli's two no-good sons, Hophni and Phinehas.

Not wasting any time, she headed to the inner court. It was within sight of Eli, whose throne in the porch probably overlooked the whole inner space.[24] "And she was in bitterness of soul, and prayed unto the LORD, and wept sore" (1 Sam. 1:10). Hannah knew she needed to bring her bitter spirit to the Lord.

Nobody can make you be a bitter person. The only person who can let bitterness into your heart is you; you are responsible for how you choose to respond. If you struggle with bitterness, here are some helps from the Bible:

- Recognize you have bitterness in your heart and bring it before the Lord (James 3:14)
- Realize you cannot be a sweet person and bitter at the same time (James 3:11)
- Wrestle the root of bitterness out of your heart before it can trouble and defile you (Heb. 12:15)
- Remove bitterness and replace it with kindness and forgiveness (Eph. 4:31-32)

I clearly remember the time I suffered from bitterness. I had been wronged, but instead of handling the situation biblically, I harbored it all inside. For several months, my bitterness consumed me. Physically, I had sleeping problems, stomach problems, and weight gain. Then I heard a terrific message on bitterness by a pastor at a teacher's conference. I realized with the help of the Holy Spirit that I was a bitter person. I remember confiding this new revelation to my roommate that night, and she said, "I know you're bitter." Talk about humbling! I didn't realize my bitterness was obvious to others. After seeking the counsel of my pastor, claiming and memorizing scripture, and crying out to the Lord for help, I can honestly say I gained victory. Though I battled bitterness for several months, through the Lord's help I gained victory; and through Him, you can do it, too.

Pouring Out Her Soul to the Lord

Hannah started praying in her heart to the Lord. "And she vowed a vow, and said, O LORD of hosts, if thou wilt indeed look on the affliction of thine handmaid, and remember me, and not forget thine handmaid, but wilt give unto thine handmaid a man child, then I will give him unto the LORD all the days of his life, and there shall no razor come upon his head" (1 Sam. 1:11). Hannah told the Lord she would dedicate her son to be a Nazarite, one who lived a separated life. While she was asking the Lord for a son, only her lips moved. Because Eli the priest didn't hear words come out of her mouth, but only saw her mouth move, he thought she was drunk.

Next thing Hannah knew during her prayer, she was being rebuked by Eli for being drunk! She could have lashed out in anger at him and reminded him his two sons were the worst offenders at the tabernacle, but she didn't. With respect for Eli and his office, she answered, "No, my lord, I am a woman of a sorrowful spirit: I have drunk neither wine nor strong drink, but have poured out my soul before the LORD" (1 Sam. 1:15).

Eli knew by her respectful reply she was not drunk. He told her, "Go in peace: and the God of Israel grant thee thy petition that thou hast asked of him" (1 Sam. 1:17). She replied, "Let thine handmaid find grace in thy sight" (1 Sam. 1:18). This was her way of asking for favor and intercessory prayer from Eli on her behalf. After she left, she ate some food, "and "her countenance was no more sad." What a relief it was that she had poured out her soul to the Lord!

Though God knows every thing that happens to you, He wants you to pour out your soul to Him. By pouring out your soul, you are showing Him you depend on Him and not on yourself. Remember that He is your Father and He takes pleasure in you confiding your problems in Him.

One of King David's secrets with his relationship with the Lord is he often took his troubles to the Lord. Many times he poured out his feelings, and the Lord favorably responded. David encourages us to do the same. He said, "Trust in him at all times; ye people, pour out your heart before him: God is a refuge for us" (Ps. 62:8).

Do you have something to complain about (Ps. 142:2)? Do you feel overwhelmed at times (Ps. 142:3)? Do you think someone is out to get you (Ps. 142:3)? Do you feel nobody cares for you (Ps. 142:4)? Do you think your enemy is stronger than you (Ps. 142:6)? Pour out your soul to the Lord. When you do, praise the Lord's name (Ps. 142:7). Remember—after you pour your soul to the Lord, praise your Lord.

Paying Back Her Vow

After rising early in the morning, Hannah and Elkanah worshipped the Lord and headed back home. In Ramah "the Lord remembered her" and Hannah conceived! What a joyous time for her and Elkanah. She had asked for a man child from the Lord and probably was confident the new life inside her was a boy.

When the midwife announced she had a boy, she "called his name Samuel, saying, Because I have asked him of the LORD" (1 Sam. 1:20). Perhaps Elkanah also had made a vow to the Lord because he went to the tabernacle to offer sacrifices "and his vow" (1 Sam. 1:21).

For reasons unknown, Hannah decided she would not go to the tabernacle with her husband until she weaned Samuel and presented him to Eli. One idea for this is that if "she took him thither, she thought she could never find in her heart to bring him back again. Note, Those who are steadfastly resolved to pay their vows may yet see good cause to defer the payment of them."[25] Perhaps Hannah didn't want to be tempted to break her vow.

It must have been bittersweet for her when it was time to take Samuel to the tabernacle. Along with packing Samuel's clothes and items, she and Elkanah brought "three bullocks, and one ephah of flour, and a bottle of wine" to offer to the Lord. They introduced Samuel to "the house of the LORD in Shiloh: and the child was young" (1 Sam. 1:24). Hannah made sure to remind Eli that she was the lady who had stood by him and prayed for a child. "For this child I prayed; and the LORD hath given me my petition which I asked of him: Therefore also I have lent him to the LORD; as long as he liveth he shall be lent to the LORD. And he worshipped the LORD there" (1 Sam. 1:27-28).

What was Hannah's response after she gave Samuel to Eli? Was she heartbroken? No, she praised the Lord! 1 Samuel 2:1-10 records her beautiful prayer, which is known as a song of praise. After she praised the Lord, she and Elkanah headed back home to Ramah, while Samuel "did minister unto the LORD before Eli the priest" (1 Sam. 2:11).

Samuel was always in Hannah's thoughts. Every year she made him a coat and brought it to him when she went to the tabernacle. When she and Elkanah would go on their yearly trip, Eli would bless them. He said, "The LORD give thee seed of this woman for the loan which is lent to the LORD" (1 Sam. 2:20). The Lord heard Eli's prayers, and she and Elkanah were blessed to have three sons and two daughters (1 Sam. 2:21). Look at how the Lord blessed Hannah and her family's life because she paid her vow to Him!

A vow is a promise you make to the Lord. Whether your vow is little or big in your eyes, it doesn't matter to God; for it is still a solemn promise made to the Lord. Besides, if you are in the habit of breaking little vows, what makes you think you can keep a big vow? God takes "no pleasure" in those who do not keep their vows. "When thou vowest a vow unto God, defer not to pay it; for he hath no pleasure in fools: pay that which thou hast vowed. Better is it that thou shouldest not vow, than that thou shouldest vow and not pay" (Eccl. 5:4-5).

Seriously consider any vow before you make it so that later on you won't reconsider it (Prov. 20:25). Because a vow will cost you something, be prepared to "pay that which thou hast vowed." If you are still determined to make the vow, write it down so you don't forget. Include where and when you made it and the circumstances as to why you made it. A spiritual journal is a good place to write down these details. It also may be helpful to write down a strategy to help keep your vow.

Please understand I'm not discouraging you from making a vow; I'm just trying to point out that a vow made to the Lord should be taken seriously. Making a vow can really change your life for the better, as seen in Hannah's case. I made a vow two years ago to the Lord that I have almost finished paying, and I couldn't even begin to tell you all the blessings I've reaped because of it.

A Lesson to Learn from Hannah

Hannah certainly had her fair share of trials and shed many tears due to her unfortunate circumstances. She could have given up on God, but instead she took her problems to Him. Her beautiful passionate prayer soon became a promise from God. In turn, she kept her promise, gave her only son back to Him, and praised Him with thanksgiving and song. She praised Him before knowing she would ever have any more children.

If you haven't been passionate about your prayer life, it's not too late to get started! Praying to the Lord is simply talking with Him. An "acrostic that works well as a prayer pattern is ACTS: A-adoration, C-confession, T-thanksgiving, and S-supplication."[26] Make it a habit to daily pray to the Lord. Ask the Lord to put a flame of passion in your heart for Him.

If you haven't been passionate about your praise life, that's not too late either! Praising the Lord is giving Him applause for who He is, what He does, and what He's going to do. "By him therefore let us offer the sacrifice of praise to God continually, that is, the fruit of our lips giving thanks to his name" (Heb. 13:15).

How did her faith affect her family?

Her faith affected her husband Elkanah. Because of Hannah's prayer and vow, he was privileged to father six children.

Her faith affected her son Samuel, who became the first prophet and even made it to the Hall of Faith in Hebrews 11:32. She made it a priority to teach and train Samuel to love the Lord. When Samuel was left at the tabernacle with Eli, he was a blessing and a help to him. We know this because every year when Hannah brought Samuel his coat, Eli would bless her to have more children. (He certainly wouldn't have encouraged her to have more children if Samuel was a troublemaker!)

Our Personal Prayer

Thank You, Lord, for hearing our prayers. May our lives be filled with a passion to love You with all our hearts. Help us to have a passion for You in our prayer life and praise life.

Questions to Consider

1. According to Acts 10:38, what will God do for those who are oppressed of the devil?

   _____

   _____

2. What steps should you take in order to get rid of bitterness in your life?

   _____

   _____

3. Is there something you need to pour out to the Lord?

   _____

   _____

4. Is there a vow you need to make or renew to the Lord?

   _____

   _____

Chapter Seven

Mary
A Woman Who Loved Her Lord Every Season of Life
Luke 1:26-52

Each season of life you are in should have a purpose and an effect. Think about the season of life you are in right now. Are you single, married, a mother with children, newly saved, a mature Christian, an empty nester, or perhaps a widow lady? Just as the four seasons of the year—spring, summer, winter, fall—accomplish different purposes and have results, the purpose of the season you are in right now should be to grow more spiritually in your love for the Lord.

Just as the seasons change, you will face many changes as you switch from one season to the next. During this time, make your love for the Lord grow stronger and stronger with each passing season. Our season of life should not separate us from loving God but draw us closer to Him. Nothing or no one, not even the powers of hell, can separate you from God's love (Rom. 8:38-39); the only person who can take away your love for God is yourself.

One thing we see from the life of Mary is that she experienced many different seasons of life, and no matter what thrills or tragedies she experienced, she always loved her Lord.

A Young Lady Who Knew Her Scripture

The city of Nazareth did not have a reputation for birthing prominent people; rather, it was home to those who lived plain, ordinary lives. A city of Galilee (Luke 1:26), Nazareth was the hometown where a young lady named Mary lived.

Mary was "espoused to a man whose name was Joseph" (Luke 1:27), meaning she was betrothed to be married. A betrothal was a contract drawn up by two families that united a son with a daughter. This was for a time of protection; and during this time, the couple was considered married. This contract was legal, and if the man or woman wanted out of the relationship, one would have to file for a divorce. After the six to twelve month betrothal period, the couple would enjoy a seven day wedding celebration. Mary was not officially united in marriage to Joseph but was excited about her upcoming marriage.

While having an ordinary day, Mary was amazed to see an angel appear right before her! The angel Gabriel said, "Hail, thou that art highly favoured, the Lord is with thee: blessed art thou among women" (Luke 1:28). Feeling troubled, Mary wondered what the angel would tell her.

Gabriel said, "Behold, thou shalt conceive in thy womb, and bring forth a son, and shalt call his name JESUS. He shall be great, and shall be called the Son of the Highest: and the Lord God shall give unto him the throne of his father David" (Luke 1:31-32).

"How shall this be, seeing I know not a man?" was Mary's reply. He explained the power of the Holy Ghost would come upon her and she would give birth to the son of God. Also, more amazing news the angel told was that her older cousin Elisabeth was six months pregnant.

"And Mary said, Behold the handmaid of the Lord; be it unto me according to thy word" (Luke 1:38). While pondering Gabriel's words, Mary knew she must visit Elisabeth; not because she lacked faith, but because she wanted her faith strengthened. Mary traveled 75 to 80 miles to get to Elisabeth's house in Judea.

When Mary saw her pregnant cousin, she happily greeted Elisabeth. As Elisabeth heard her greeting, Elisabeth's baby leaped inside her womb. Filled with the Holy Ghost, Elisabeth loudly proclaimed a blessing on Mary's life.

After Elisabeth's blessing, Mary joyfully praised the Lord. "My soul doth magnify the Lord" (Luke 1:46). She went on to quote what is known as "The Magnificat" (Luke 1:46-55). In the Magnificat there are "15 discernible quotations from the OT...showing how much the OT was known."[27] After staying with Elisabeth for three months, Mary headed back to her own house.

To make reference to fifteen Old Testament verses shows Mary knew the Scripture, favoring verses from Psalms. Sometime throughout her life she had made it a priority to hide God's Word in her heart. Memorizing God's Word and hiding it in your heart will keep you from sinning (Ps. 119:11), give you an offensive weapon to ward off attacks from the devil (Eph. 6:17), reveal what you delight in (Ps. 1:2), and give you life (Matt. 4:4).

Memorizing God's Word will take time, effort, and initiative. If the "word of God is quick, and powerful, and sharper than any twoedged sword" (Heb. 4:12), shouldn't we desire to have it in our hearts?

The importance of memorizing verses is illustrated in *Evidence Not Seen*, the story of a young missionary lady named Darliene Diebler, who was imprisoned by the Japanese during World War II. She wasn't allowed the luxury of having a Bible with her during some of her imprisonment. However, many verses she had memorized prior to this time were a strength and help in her time of need. Since we don't know if we will ever be in an awful situation without our Bible, it's important to hide God's Word in our hearts now.

A First-Time Mother Living in a Faraway Place and Close to God

When Mary arrived back in Nazareth, she informed Joseph that she was pregnant—this news was so shocking to Joseph! By law, he could have had her stoned for being pregnant (Deut. 22:21). Joseph left, wondering if he should divorce her. That night in a dream, the angel Gabriel told him not to be afraid—Mary was going to give birth to the

Messiah (Matt. 1:20-23)! After Joseph awoke the next morning, he hurried to Mary's house to tell her he was ready to marry her.

Meanwhile, to fulfill a prophecy in Micah 5:2, the spirit of God moved upon Caesar Augustus to make a royal decree. Known in the history books as Octavian, in 27 B.C., he was given the title Caesar Augustus by the Roman senate. Caesar is a generic word for king and Augustus means "revered one." He announced that everybody would be taxed (Luke 2:1), and families needed to register their family names. The Jews hated to pay taxes to the Romans. One reason is Caesar's image was on the coins, and they viewed these coins as idol worship.[28] Because Joseph was from the house of David, he was required to go to Bethlehem, meaning a very-pregnant Mary would have to say good-bye to her friends and family.

Though Bethlehem was to the south of Nazareth, Joseph and Mary "went up from Galilee" (Luke 2:4). After they headed down the hill Nazareth was located, they arrived in a valley. From that valley, they climbed *up* 2,564 feet in elevation to get to Bethlehem. The terrain was very rocky and it was about a 90 mile trip.

Because Joseph and Mary arrived to a city packed with people, "there was no room for them in the inn." Shortly after they arrived, Jesus was born and Mary "wrapped him in swaddling clothes, and laid him in a manger" (Luke 2:7). (A manger was a feed trough for animals and is why we assume they stayed in a stable.).

Later that night, shepherds appeared at their humble dwelling. Mary and Joseph were amazed when the shepherds told them angels appeared to them and praised Jesus' birth (Luke 2:16-18); Mary "pondered these things in her heart" (Luke 2:19). She loved being a new mother and eight days later, Jesus was circumcised and officially named. Though she was far away from her home of Nazareth, Mary was close to God because she was where He wanted her to be.

When you are where God wants you to be, He is close to you no matter how far away everyone else may be. "And the LORD, he it is that doth go before thee; he will be with thee, he will not fail thee, neither forsake thee: fear not, neither be dismayed" (Deut. 31:8). Some other great verses on the Lord being with you when you are with Him: Josh. 1:5-9; Ps. 73:23; Ps. 91; Is. 43:2; Acts 1:8.

Jesus promised He will be with us **always** when we are doing what He wants us to do. Before He ascended to heaven, He told His disciples to go into the world and teach others about Him. Then He made His promise, "And, lo, I am with you alway, even unto the end of the world" (Matt. 28:20). It is when we follow Him, doing what He wants us to do, that we can have assurance He is with us.

A Mother Who Took Her Children to God's House

Mary was excited as she, Joseph, and 40-day-old Jesus, headed to the temple in Jerusalem (Luke 2:22). She had just finished her days of purification (a law stating in Lev. 12:4 that any mother who gave birth to a boy had to wait forty days to participate in any ceremonies) and brought along her sacrifice of two turtledoves or two pigeons. Perhaps she wished she could have afforded to bring a lamb—but wait—she had brought Jesus, the "Lamb of God" (John 1:29).

A man named Simeon approached Mary, Joseph, and Jesus. He took baby Jesus in his arms and blessed God, blessed Mary and Joseph, and prophesied Jesus' doings (Luke 2:29-35). Continuing to speak, he said to Mary, "Yea, a sword shall pierce through thy own soul also" (Luke 2:35). He knew Mary would experience pain as Jesus' mother. After Simeon spoke, a widow named Anna appeared and thanked God for sending Jesus.

Meanwhile, wise men had seen a star shine in the East, and after a long trip, headed to the palace in Jerusalem to worship a king. Instead, they saw King Herod who was jealous when he heard about their search. When the wise men arrived at Mary and Joseph's home, they presented gifts of gold, frankincense, and myrrh to baby Jesus (Matt. 2:11). After they left, Mary was woken by Joseph in the middle of the night; he told her they needed to leave Bethlehem immediately. An angel had warned Joseph in a dream that King Herod was looking for the Messiah and was going to kill all Jewish baby boys around two years old (Matt. 2:14).

Joseph and Mary probably used the gifts the wise men gave them to cover the costs for their escape. It took them many weeks to travel to Egypt (possibly a 175 mile trip). Egypt was known as a place of refuge for the Jewish people, and even around 150 B.C. the Jews had their own temple built.[29] Still, Mary must have been so glad when Joseph informed her King Herod was dead and they could travel back to Israel (they were in Egypt for probably several months). Then, Joseph was told in another dream to go north to Galilee because a wicked ruler named Archelaus, Herod's son, was reigning in Judea (the southern part of Israel) (Matt. 2:22).

Go to Galilee! Joseph and Mary would be able to raise their growing family in Nazareth. It was there Jesus "grew, and waxed strong in spirit, filled with wisdom: and the grace of God was upon him" (Luke 2:40). Mary knew she would never forget the time when the family and twelve-year-old Jesus went to Jerusalem to celebrate the Passover. What follows might be the way Mary would tell the story.

He had been excited about going to the temple. Different from most children, He enjoyed listening to the rabbis talk about God. When the festivities were over, as our family made our way home, we discovered Jesus wasn't with us. After searching three days, we found Him in the temple (Luke 2:42-46), talking and listening to the rabbis. I scolded Him for causing me and Joseph to worry. Jesus reminded me He was to be about His Father's business. Though I didn't understand His answer, at the time, I "kept all these sayings" in my heart (Luke 2:51). I reminded myself I was glad He loved being at the temple.

Like Mary, we need to take our children to our place of worship. As mothers and Christians, we are to "provoke unto love and to good works: Not forsaking the assembling of ourselves together, as the manner of some is; but exhorting one another: and so much the more, as ye see the day approaching" (Heb. 10:24-25). We are to provoke (encourage) others (like our children) to love the Lord and His house.

When your children have a love for God's house, have them put their love into action for His house. The house of God will need repairs, cleaning, decorating, and organizing. It is important they are taught to have a love for God's house; if not, they may try to destroy it (2 Chron. 24:7). Time and effort by God's people are necessary to maintain a house worthy of God's presence.

If possible, take your children to God's house from the very beginning of their lives. If your children are older and you just started attending church, start where you are. Ground and plant their hearts in God's house. "Those that be planted in the house of the LORD shall flourish in the courts of our God" (Ps. 92:13). If you're not planting their feet in God's house, what soil are their feet planted in?

A Mature Mother Who Prayed to Her Lord

Other children Mary and Joseph had were James, Joses, Juda (Jude), Simon, and unnamed sisters. When Jesus started His public ministry at the age of 30, though He was popular with multitudes of people, His own brethren were offended by Him (Mark 6:3-4). Mary would bring His brethren to hear Him speak (Luke 8:19), and yet, "neither did his brethren believe in him" (John 7:5).

Mary's love for Jesus brought her joy and pain. When He was being crucified on the cross, she witnessed His humiliation, pain, and death. Though she saw the spear pierce His side, the blood trickling from the crown of thorns, the nails poking into His hands and feet, the angry crowd yelling insults—she stood by Him, loving Him (John 19:25). (Many scholars believe she was a widow because there is no mention of Joseph at the cross.)

Three days later, the city shook with excitement when they heard Jesus had risen from the dead. Perhaps this was when Jesus' brethren believed He was the Son of God and followed Him. Forty days later when Jesus ascended into heaven, Mary, His brethren, and other disciples gathered in Jerusalem to pray. "These all continued with one accord in prayer and supplication, with the women, and Mary the mother of Jesus, and with his brethren" (Acts 1:14). .

Leonard Ravenhill wrote, "Poverty stricken as the church is today in many things, she is most stricken here, in the place of prayer.

We have many organizers, but few agonizers; many players and payers, but few prayers; many singers, few clingers; lots of pastors, but few wrestlers; many fears, few tears; much fashion, little passion; many interferers, few intercessors; many writers, but few fighters. Failing here, we fail everywhere."[30]

Prayer is powerful. Remember, you need power from the Lord to defeat the devil. After the armor of God is listed in Ephesians 6:13-17, we are exhorted to pray "always" (Eph. 6:18). No matter what season of life you are in, you can pray. A consistent prayer life in the season of life you are in will carry over throughout every season (hopefully growing stronger) and keep you in communion with your Lord.

If we were aware of the power of prayer like the devil is aware, we would be on our knees more. "No one is a firmer believer in the power of prayer than the devil; not that he practices it, but he suffers from it" (Guy H. King).[31] Don't be content with your prayer life. Make every effort to continually strengthen your relationship with the Lord.

A Lesson to Learn from Mary

You won't find a verse that says, "And Mary loved her Lord," but by looking at her life we know she did. From young girl to older widow, Mary's love for her Lord was seen through her actions. It is this type of love God wants you to have for Him. Jesus reminds us the first commandment is that we should love the Lord with all our heart, soul, mind, and strength (Mark 12:30).

If you haven't loved the Lord in your previous seasons of life, determine that you will love Him today and for the rest of your life. If you have loved the Lord in every season, continue to love Him! Like any relationship, loving someone will take energy and time. When we sow seeds of love for the Lord and others, we will reap a life of love. "And let us not be weary in well doing: for in due season we shall reap, if we faint not" (Gal. 6:9).

How did her faith affect her family?

Her faith affected her husband Joseph. It was her love for God, even as a young child, that gave her favor with God for her to be chosen to bear the Messiah. This great honor had a huge impact in Joseph's life, bringing him great privilege and responsibility.

Her faith affected her other children. We do not know how many of them believed in Jesus, though we know two did: James and Jude. James was the author of the book of James, and Jude was the writer of the book of Jude. When "Jesus' brethren" were mentioned in scripture, so was their mother, Mary. As she brought them to hear Jesus and prayed with them after His ascension, her life influenced them to love Her Lord.

Our Personal Prayer

We love You, Lord. As we enter into different seasons of life, help our love to continually grow for You. At the end of our life, we want to look back and see we have done great things for You because of our love for You.

Questions to Consider

1. In the season of life you are in, how can you show your love for the Lord?

    _____

    _____

2. When's the last time you memorized a Bible verse? Pick a verse to memorize and write how it can help you.

    _____

    _____

3. Is there someone you know who needs to come to church? How can you help him come?

_____

_____

4. Are you content with your prayer life? Please explain.

_____

_____

Chapter Eight

Rebekah

A Woman Who Had a Great Start In Life But a Lousy Finish

Genesis 24-27

One parable spoken by Jesus is about a man who wanted to build a tower. However, this man didn't calculate how much it would cost to build. After the foundation was laid, he realized he wouldn't be able to finish it. People quickly noticed nothing was happening after the foundation and began to make fun of the guy. They said, "Look at what he started to build but wasn't able to finish!" (Luke 14:28-30).

It's not how you start but how you finish that counts. What if I had started this chapter, never finished it, and then printed it in this book? You could read it but you would be missing the end of the story and the whole picture. The same is true in your life. If you start serving the Lord but then quit sometime along the way, you will be missing out on the story God wants your life to write and others to read.

If you started out doing good things for the Lord, keep it up. Don't be fooled into thinking that just because you're serving the Lord today means you will be two days from now. If you haven't been serving the Lord lately, get up and get going. Ask yourself: *What am I doing for the Lord today?* You don't need to be like Rebekah, who had a great start in life, but unfortunately had a lousy finish.

Taking the Initiative

After Abraham passed the test of offering his son Isaac to the Lord on Mt. Moriah, he was told his seed would multiply as the stars of the sky (Gen. 22:15-17). When Abraham returned home, he heard about his family who lived in Nahor. Perhaps hearing that his nephew Bethuel had a daughter named Rebekah (Gen. 22:23) started his thinking about whom Isaac should marry.

When Isaac was 40 years old, Abraham decided to send his trusted servant Eliezer to his home country to find Isaac a wife. After the 500-mile trip, Eliezer and his ten camels arrived at a well outside the city of Nahor. There, he specifically asked the Lord to send an available young lady to give water to him and his camels (Gen. 24:14).

Before he finished his prayer, Rebekah came walking to the well with a pitcher in her hand. After she filled her pitcher with water, Eliezer approached the beautiful young woman and asked for some water. She quickly gave him water and offered to draw water for the camels, also! "It has been estimated that she perhaps drew 30-60 gallons of water for the camels to drink."[32] It is possible she probably gave the servants with Eliezer water too (Gen. 24:32).

She must have been surprised when Eliezer presented her with a golden earring and two bracelets (Gen. 24:22)! When Eliezer discovered her family was related to Abraham's family and he was invited to stay at her house, he bowed his head and worshipped the Lord (Gen. 24:24-25). He knew by Rebekah getting all that water for his camels that she had initiative.

Initiative is when you see something that needs to be done and do it without being asked. I like the saying, "When you see the need, take the lead."[33] People who take the initiative are a help and a blessing to others.

An ant is commended for taking the initiative, and we are exhorted by the wisest man who ever lived to learn from it. "Go to the ant, thou sluggard; consider her ways, and be wise: Which having no guide, overseer, or ruler, Provideth her meat in the summer, and gathereth her food in the harvest" (Prov. 6:6-8). The ant has no ruler, but still sees what needs to be done and does it.

You may not see anything needing to be done at your church, but I'll bet you're not looking too hard. You may not see something that needs to change in your life, but start looking. You must first *see* something before you do something. And when you *do* that something, you are taking initiative.

Displaying Great Courage

Rebekah ran home, eager to tell her family what happened and show them her new jewelry. Her brother Laban was the first to see her jewelry and hear her story. His greedy heart was impressed and he hurried to prepare accommodations for Eliezer, the camels, and his servants (Gen. 24:32).

Before eating, Eliezer explained about Abraham, the mission he had, and how God sent Rebekah to him (Gen. 24:48). Bethuel, Rebekah's dad, and Laban agreed it was God's will for Rebekah to marry Isaac. Did Rebekah know her entire future was being discussed? Finally she was presented with beautiful jewelry and clothes from Eliezer and knew she was to be married.

The next morning her mother and brother informed Eliezer they wanted Rebekah to stay for ten more days. However, they let Rebekah make the final decision and she said, "I will go" (Gen. 24:58). Her answer indicated good character qualities of decisiveness and trust. Everyone quickly prepared with the packing for Rebekah, her nurse Deborah, and her servants. After being given a blessing, she and her servants rode away on camels brought by Eliezer.

When they arrived on Abraham's property, Rebekah was on the lookout for her new husband. She spotted a man and asked Eliezer, "What man is this that walketh in the field to meet us? And the servant had said, It is my master: therefore she took a vail, and covered herself" (Gen. 24:65). This revealed she was modest and submissive. I like that she hopped off her camel to meet him, turning an awkward situation into something very beautiful. Eliezer made the introductions to Isaac (I'm sure he was only half-listening!), and Isaac claimed Rebekah to be his bride.

It took courage on Rebekah's part to leave her family to marry a guy she didn't know. Courage is not a quality only men should have, but all ladies, as well. We are all commanded to have courage. "Have not I commanded thee? Be strong and of a good courage; be not afraid, neither be thou dismayed: for the LORD thy God is with thee whithersoever thou goest" (Josh. 1:9).

Courage is displaying hope and trust in the Lord. "Wait on the LORD: be of good courage, and he shall strengthen thine heart: wait, I say, on the LORD" (Ps. 27:14). When we have courage, it is then the Lord will give us strength. "Be of good courage, and he shall strengthen your heart" (Ps. 31:24).

Ask the Lord to give you courage to make right decisions. It takes courage to stand with your husband and against your family at times. It takes courage to show and tell your convictions. It takes courage to confront somebody that wronged you. It takes courage to go out and tell others about Jesus. You must have courage for your Lord, and when you do He will give you strength.

Displaying Impatience with God's Timing

After Rebekah and Isaac married, they hoped to have children. Though Rebekah's womb was barren, her new mother-in-law, Keturah, had no problem giving Abraham six boys (Gen. 25:1). Isaac's brothers were given gifts by Abraham, but it was Isaac to whom Abraham gave all that he had. After Abraham died, Isaac received more blessings from the Lord (Gen. 25:11). When they had been married for nineteen years, Isaac asked the Lord to bless them with a child.

Soon afterward, Rebekah found out she was pregnant with not one baby, but two! She asked the Lord why the two babies fought in her womb; God explained that each baby represented a nation and the older child would serve the younger (Gen. 25:23).When her delivery time came, covered with red hair Esau came out first, his heel gripped by the hand of his younger brother, whom they named Jacob (meaning cheater).

Rebekah instantly favored smooth-skinned Jacob and Isaac favored hairy Esau. Soon Esau became a hunter while Jacob enjoyed working around the house. One day, after Esau came back from a hunting trip he begged for some red lentil soup that Jacob had made. Jacob told him he would give him soup only if Esau gave him his birthright. Esau agreed to the deal, but later felt cheated (in Gen. 27:36 he claimed Jacob had stolen the birthright).

More troubles happened, the first being a famine in the land. They moved to Gerar, and there Isaac wanted people to think he and Rebekah were brother and sister so his life wouldn't be in danger (Gen. 26:7). Thankfully, the Lord intervened in the situation and they returned home. The second trouble came after Esau, who had turned 40, married two heathen women (Gen. 26:34).

When Rebekah and Isaac had been married for 97 years (making Isaac to be 137 years old),[34] Isaac's eyesight and physical health were failing and Rebekah carried the load of taking care of him. "With Isaac's health failing, Rebekah probably became insecure and felt she had to start taking control."[35]

One day, while Isaac had a talk with Esau, Rebekah made sure to eavesdrop on their conversation. Isaac told Esau to go hunting and make him some venison to eat, for he was ready to give Esau the blessing. When Esau left, Rebekah hurried to tell Jacob what he needed to do. "Now therefore, my son, obey my voice according to that which I command thee. Go now to the flock, and fetch me from thence two good kids of the goats; and I will make them savoury meat for thy father, such as he loveth" (Gen. 27:8-9).

Jacob protested the plan wouldn't work and expressed concern he would be caught. "My father peradventure will feel me, and I shall seem to him as a deceiver; and I shall bring a curse upon me, and not a blessing. And his mother said unto him, Upon me be thy curse, my son: only obey my voice, and go fetch me them" (Gen. 27:12-13).

Her impatience with God's timing caused her to take matters into her own hands. Just because God had told her the older son would serve the younger son didn't justify her evil conduct to "help God." "Her plan was a signal offense against God in many ways, but chiefly in the sinful impatience it displayed, in the foolish supposition that his sovereign designs needed the assistance of, or could be helped by, human craft in the shape of female cunning (Whitelaw)."[36]

We must have patience with God's timing. A patient lady will endure and wait on the Lord; an impatient lady may wait for a little while but will soon take matters into her own hands. Springing from selfishness, impatience makes us want to hurry something along so that we can gain from it.

How can we acquire patience? Patience is a result of enduring trials and temptations. "But we glory in tribulations also: knowing that tribulation worketh patience" (Rom. 5:3). Though trials are hard to go through, you can learn patience from your trial—making some good come from the trial. "Knowing this, that the trying of your faith worketh patience. But let patience have her perfect work, that ye may be perfect and entire, wanting nothing" (James 1:3-4).

Hebrews 12:1 says we are to run our race "with patience." An impatient runner may not have the endurance to finish her race, but a patient runner will eventually reach the finish line. Are you impatient about something right now? Be patient with God's timing; we must want for His will to be done His way and in His time.

Underestimating the Cost of Her Sin

Rebekah busily prepared the two goats Jacob brought her. She went to get clothes she kept for Esau in her house, put them on Jacob, and put the goat skins on his hands and neck. No doubt she watched and listened as Jacob took the prepared meat and went before Isaac.

Smooth Jacob (in more ways than one) pulled the whole scheme off by deceiving his father and stealing Esau's blessing. After Jacob left, Esau appeared before his father with his savory meat, but discovered Jacob had stolen his blessing. When Isaac told Esau that he would serve his younger brother, Esau was furious! He threatened to kill Jacob after their father died.

Rebekah told Jacob, "Now therefore, my son, obey my voice; and arise, flee thou to Laban my brother to Haran; And tarry with him a few days, until thy brother's fury turn away; Until thy brother's anger turn away from thee, and he forget that which thou hast done to him: then I will send, and fetch thee from thence: why should I be deprived also of you both in one day?" (Gen. 27:43-45). Did she really think Esau wouldn't be angry in a few days?

Still controlling the situation, Rebekah went to Isaac and hinted she hoped Jacob wouldn't marry one of the local heathen girls like Esau did. "I am weary of my life because of the daughters of Heth: if Jacob take a wife of the daughters of Heth...what good shall my life do me?" (Gen. 27:46). Her words were true, but her real motive was to have Isaac send Jacob away to keep him from harm.

Isaac called Jacob to bless him (Gen. 28:1) and give him some advice. Though Rebekah's family lived far away, Isaac told Jacob to go there and live with her family. After Jacob left, Rebekah probably thought she would see him again—but she never did; she was dead by the time Jacob returned home 20 years later. Amazingly, it was Isaac who was still alive; he lived 43 years later and died at the age of 180. She underestimated the cost her sin would have on her and her family.

Like the foolish builder underestimated the cost for his project (Luke 14:28), don't underestimate the cost of your sin. Sin controls (Rom. 6:12), deceives and destroys (Rom. 7:11), and enslaves (Rom. 7:14). Thankfully, Jesus Christ counted the cost of our sin and willingly paid the price (Rom. 6:9-10). Instead of serving sin, focus on serving your Savior.

Sarah Carlson, in her book *Ready or Not*, wrote about sin-spiders. Just like we ladies would panic if there were a spider hanging on our shoulder, we should have the same reaction to sin that's hanging over us. "If you have many ugly, hairy spiders living on your shoulder, you are going to be weighed down...In the same way, if you are not angry at your sin, you will continue to have it and love it. You will not possibly be able to do what God wants you to do—now or later."[37]

Don't think you can play with sin and not pay any price. Your sin can hurt you and others more than you will ever realize. The pleasures of sin last a few days (Heb. 11:25), but the punishment of sin can last your entire lifetime.[38] "Then when lust hath conceived, it bringeth forth sin: and sin, when it is finished, bringeth forth death" (James 1:15). Sin will never bring a happy ending to anyone's life.

A Lesson to Learn from Rebekah

What happened to the lady who had all the great character qualities at the beginning? Her initiative for doing right turned to doing wrong; her courage turned to making the wrong decisions out of fear; her unselfishness turned to selfishness; her outward beauty turned to inward ugliness because of her sin. She gave up maintaining her spiritual life and let her own selfish desires control her decisions.

The apostle Paul compares the Christian life to a race. Though his race in life had a lousy start, he had an awesome finish. "For I am now ready to be offered, and the time of my departure is at hand. I have fought a good fight, I have finished my course, I have kept the faith" (2 Tim. 4:6-7). May you stay on your race track or get up and running again so that you, too, can have an awesome finish for your Lord.

How did her faith affect her family?

Her faith affected her husband Isaac. In the beginning, her unselfishness to leave right away with Eliezer affected Isaac for the good. Unfortunately, her selfishness in the end brought a wedge between them.

Her faith affected her son Esau. Aside from his own mother scheming against him, she could have made an effort to have been a godly influence in the life of his wives. "Rebekah's sin affected the whole family…We are not an island unto ourselves."[39]

Her faith affected her son Jacob. "Her [Rebekah's] craftiness was certainly reproduced in her son Jacob."[40] She had taught him to lie and deceive. Jacob sowed deceit and would later reap deceit from his father-in-law, wives, and ten sons.

Our Personal Prayer

Lord, we do desire to start doing things right for You. Though we will be weary at times, help us to stay on course of our race. May we finish our race with joy, and may it bring glory to You.

Questions to Consider

1. Are you lacking some good character qualities you used to have in your life? How can you bring those back?

   _____

   _____

2. What is an area in your life you need to have courage?

   _____

   _____

3. How can selfishness be dangerous in your life and others?

   _____

   _____

4. According to Acts 20:24, how are you supposed to finish your course?

   _____

   _____

Chapter Nine

Ruth

A Woman Whose Friendship Was a Blessing

Ruth 1-4

"Friendship is rare; loneliness is common."[41] Why is a good friendship rare? It's because a good friendship takes time and energy. But, oh, the blessings! A good friend will be a help, an encouragement, and a blessing. "Two are better than one; because they have a good reward for their labour. For if they fall, the one will lift up his fellow: but woe to him that is alone when he falleth; for he hath not another to help him up" (Ecc. 4:9-10).

Giving someone the gift of friendship is a higher value than a necklace she might want from a jewelry store. What comfort is a necklace to a hurting, lonely soul? None. The name Ruth means "friend" and Ruth indeed lived up to the meaning of her name by choosing to be her mother-in-law's friend. And because she chose to be a friend, her friendship was a blessing to someone else.

Offering Friendship to a Needful Lady

The Israelites were not friends with the Moabites. The reason dated back to when the Israelites, under Moses' leadership, escaped from Egypt and tried to go through Moab to get to the Promised Land. However, the Moabites refused to allow them in their country and withheld food or aid. Because of this, the Israelites cursed them and refused to allow Moabites to enter into the Israelite congregations. Later, the Moabites hired a man named Balaam to curse the Israelites (Deut. 23:3-4).

Ruth was one of only a few Moabites who converted to Judaism. In her town of Moab she met an Israelite family that had traveled there to escape a famine. The father, Elimelech, brought his wife, Naomi, and two sons, Mahlon and Chilion. Shortly afterward, Elimelech died and Ruth married his older son Mahlon; Chilion also married a Moabite girl named Orpah (Ruth 1:1-4). It is possible Mahlon was a sickly man, for his name means "infirmity or puny."

Ruth was still childless in their marriage ten years later. It was a sad day when she heard that Mahlon and her brother-in-law died. Later, when Naomi knew there was no longer a famine in Israel, she decided to move back. Ruth and Orpah headed to Israel with Naomi. On the way, Naomi asked her two daughters-in-law to return to their home, for she knew she could never give them another husband. After hearing that, Orpah left. Ruth was not swayed by Naomi's speech but "clave to her."

"And Ruth said, Intreat me not to leave thee, or to return from following after thee: for whither thou goest, I will go; and where thou lodgest, I will lodge: thy people shall be my people, and thy God my God: Where thou diest, will I die, and there will I be buried: the LORD do so to me, and more also, if ought but death part thee and me" (Ruth 1:16-17). When Naomi saw Ruth meant her offer of friendship, she let her come along.

Growing up an Army brat, I learned that in order to have friends I had to be friendly. In most places where I lived, I always had a close friend. Yet, I still remember when I was a sophomore in high school and didn't have a close friend. The reason? I wasn't very friendly. I guess you could say I had given up because I knew we would be moving again in nine months and didn't want to go through the whole "say hello then goodbye" routine. Don't get me wrong—I got along well with everybody at school and at church, but I didn't have a close friend—which was my fault. It probably goes without saying, but that was the worst year of my life. I remember being at a Christian camp and making a resolution that wherever we moved I would be friendly and make a good friend. I even prayed for my unknown friend, and I'm happy to say I made an awesome friend when we moved again. Nineteen years later, in fact, that friend and I are still close.

You must be a friend to others if you want to have a friend. Take the initiative and make the first move—whether it's an email, call, or a simple hello. "A man that hath friends must shew himself friendly" (Prov. 18:24). Instead of sitting around and complaining about having no friends, do something. Ask the Lord to send you a close friend; then be the right friend to that person.

Working Hard to be a Help

In April, and the beginning of barley harvest, Ruth and Naomi arrived in Bethlehem. Their arrival created quite a stir so that "all the city was moved about them" (Ruth 1:19). People were wondering if it was really Naomi walking with the Moabitess. Naomi acknowledged that she was who they thought she was, but asked them to call her Mara (meaning bitter) instead of Naomi (meaning pleasant). She explained that she felt empty because of the loss of her husband and two sons.

Ruth wasted no time sight seeing. Instead, she told Naomi, "Let me now go to the field, and glean ears of corn after him in whose sight I shall find grace. And she said unto her, Go, my daughter" (Ruth 2:2). (Corn in this verse signifies a type of grain—which at this time is barley.) After she had been gleaning for awhile, a man of importance approached her.

He told her to keep working in his field and he would take care of her needs. Ruth was stunned! "Then she fell on her face, and bowed herself to the ground, and said unto him, Why have I found grace in thine eyes, that thou shouldest take knowledge of me, seeing I am a stranger?" (Ruth 2:10). Being a "stranger" (foreigner), Ruth was aware of hostilities towards the Moabite people.

Boaz said, "It hath fully been shewed me, all that thou hast done unto thy mother in law since the death of thine husband: and how thou hast left thy father and thy mother, and the land of thy nativity, and art come unto a people which thou knewest not heretofore" (Ruth 2:11).

Boaz's friendly words comforted her, and after eating dinner with him, she hurried back to work. She did not know Boaz had told the workers to leave some "handfuls of purpose" (Ruth 2:16) of barley for her. After gleaning seven gallons of barley, she beat it with a stick and headed home.

Returning to Naomi that night, she showed her mother-in-law the barley. Shocked at the great amount, Naomi asked her whose field she worked. When Naomi heard Ruth say it was Boaz's field, she praised the Lord and excitedly informed Ruth that Boaz was a near kinsman (in plain English—husband material!). Naomi advised Ruth to work only in Boaz's field, which she did until the end of the wheat harvest (about the end of May).

A great illustration of a hard working woman is the virtuous woman in Proverbs 31. "She seeketh wool, and flax, and worketh willingly with her hands" (Prov. 31:13). "She girdeth her loins with strength, and strengtheneth her arms" (Prov. 31:17).

Don't mistake hard work with busyness. Busyness can be a result of lack of planning or a lack of priorities; a hard worker has a goal and works toward that goal. Remember—don't compare what you do with other ladies. Your goals won't be the same as theirs; just make sure you work hard at what you need to do.

Not only do we see the Virtuous Woman constantly in action, but we also see the results of her action. "Her children arise up, and call her blessed; her husband also, and he praiseth her" (Prov. 31:28). When we work hard at everything we do, it will be a benefit to others.

Being a Virtuous Woman

After Ruth finished working in the fields, Naomi the matchmaker advised Ruth to go meet Boaz that night at the threshing floor. "Wash thyself therefore, and anoint thee, and put thy raiment upon thee, and get thee down to the floor: but make not thyself known unto the man, until he shall have done eating and drinking. And it shall be, when he lieth down, that thou shalt mark the place where he shall lie, and thou shalt go in, and uncover his feet, and lay thee down; and he will tell thee what thou shalt do" (Ruth 3:3-4). Not even hesitating, Ruth agreed to Naomi's plan.

While lying at Boaz's feet that night, Boaz asked, "Who are you?" She answered, "I am Ruth thine handmaid: spread therefore thy skirt over thine handmaid; for thou art a near kinsman" (Ruth 3:9). Her answer to him indicated she desired to marry him! Though her actions may seem strange to us, she was acting in accordance to the law in Deuteronomy 25:5-10.

Can you imagine how she must have wondered what Boaz's reaction would be? Feeling pleased, Boaz blessed Ruth and praised her for her kindness. "And now, my daughter, fear not; I will do to thee all that thou requirest: for all the city of my people doth know that thou art a virtuous woman" (Ruth 3:11). He informed her someone else in the family was a nearer kinsman, but maybe the nearer kinsman would agree to let Boaz marry her.

Still unsure of her future, Ruth lay back down at Boaz's feet. When she arose early in the morning, Boaz took her veil and gave her six measures of barley. (Scholars are unsure about the quantity of six measures, but many believe it equaled about 15 gallons! She probably wound all that barley in her veil and put it on her head to carry. "It is well known that women can carry great weights when duly positioned on their heads."[42])

When Ruth arrived at her house, the first question out of Naomi's mouth was, "Who art thou, my daughter?" Are you Mrs. Boaz now? Should I start planning a bridal shower? Ruth told her what happened, and Naomi advised her to wait patiently (Ruth 3:18). Naomi knew Boaz would take care of the details and want to marry Ruth, for she was a virtuous woman.

A virtuous woman is a good treasure for any man to find. "Who can find a virtuous woman? for her price is far above rubies" (Prov. 31:10). The word virtuous means "a force, an army, strength." The first two attributes listed for the virtuous woman are trustworthiness and kindness (Prov. 31:11-12).

Though we praise the Virtuous Woman for all that she did, it's really her inner spirit that enabled her to do so much. If you copied just her actions, you wouldn't necessarily be considered a virtuous woman. Planting a garden, learning how to make clothes, and getting involved in real estate are all great things to learn and do, but they are just things. They will not turn you into a virtuous woman.

The secret to the virtuous woman in Proverbs 31 is not her blue-ribbon accomplishments but her inner strength. "Strength and honour are her clothing; and she shall rejoice in time to come" (Prov. 31:25). It is your inner strength that defines who you are, and never forget your inner strength comes from the Lord.

Building a House for the Lord

While Ruth stayed with Naomi, Boaz headed to the gate. When he spotted the man who was the nearer kinsman to Ruth, he called him over. After calling ten witnesses, he informed the kinsman that Naomi's property needed to be redeemed. The kinsman wanted the property, but decided against the deal when he heard he would have to marry Ruth.

Boaz was granted permission to buy the land and marry Ruth. The kinsman said, "Buy it for thee" (Ruth 4:8), took off his shoe, and handed it to Boaz. Boaz turned to the ten witnesses and told them he would buy all that was Naomi's and marry Ruth. All the people and elders happily told Boaz they were witnesses and then blessed his house.

"The LORD make the woman that is come into thine house like Rachel and like Leah, which two did build the house of Israel: and do thou worthily in Ephratah, and be famous in Bethlehem: And let thy house be like the house of Pharez, whom Tamar bare unto Judah, of the seed which the LORD shall give thee of this young woman" (Ruth 4:11-12).

Ruth happily married Boaz and was pleased to give him a son. Naomi was thrilled to finally be a grandmother! When her friends saw her, they said, "Blessed be the LORD, which hath not left thee this day without a kinsman, that his name may be famous in Israel. And he shall

90

be unto thee a restorer of thy life, and a nourisher of thine old age: for thy daughter in law, which loveth thee, which is better to thee than seven sons, hath born him" (Ruth 4:14-15). (What a compliment for Ruth to be better than seven sons!)

"And Naomi took the child, and laid it in her bosom, and became nurse unto it" (Ruth 4:16). The Hebrew word for nurse here is *aman* which means "to nourish, foster as a parent." Naomi was not a wet nurse like some believe (that Hebrew word for nurse would be *yanaq*, meaning "to suck or give milk").

It appears Naomi named her grandson Obed, meaning "servant," from the advice of her neighbors! Ruth and Boaz agreed to the name and no doubt encouraged Obed to live up to his name. Later on, "Obed begat Jesse, and Jesse begat David" (Ruth 4:22).

This made Ruth to be King David's great grandmother and part of the lineage of Christ. The lineage is listed in the first chapter of Matthew; Ruth's name is listed with two other ladies, Tamar and Rahab, and a reference to Bathsheba as the wife of Uriah. No other ladies names are listed with the men (with the exception of Mary at the end) like Sarah or Rebekah. These four women are comprised of two prostitutes, a Moabitess, and an adulteress—not exactly an ideal family tree, but the houses built by these ladies were blessed by the Lord.

It is a wise lady who places a priority on building her house. "Every wise woman buildeth her house" (Prov. 14:1)—not building a house literally with tools, but figuratively. God has given you "tools" to help manage your household well and efficiently. Two of those tools are wisdom and understanding. "Through wisdom is an house builded; and by understanding it is established" (Prov. 24:3).

For your house to last against the storms of the world, you must make sure it is built on the foundation of the Lord Jesus. No matter how good looking or sturdy a house is built, it will fall if not on a solid foundation (Luke 6:49).

Put the Lord first in everything you do in your house, and He will bless your house. "Now therefore let it please thee to bless the house of thy servant, that it may be before thee for ever: for thou blessest, O LORD, and it shall be blessed for ever" (1 Chron. 17:27).

A Lesson to Learn from Ruth

Ruth was a giver, an initiator; look at all the blessings she reaped—a wonderful husband, a baby boy, a great relationship with Naomi, being included into the Israelite community, and a legacy that lived. The Lord blessed her life because she was such a blessing to others.

While you are being a friend to others, don't forget to nurture your friendship with the Lord. Did you know you can have an intimate friendship with Him (see Ex. 33:11 and James 2:23)? Your friendship with Him will bless your life in so many ways.

Though friendships take time and energy, you will not regret giving yourself to others and to your Lord. I encourage you to grow in your friendship with the Lord; I encourage you to reach out to someone. As you offer the gift of friendship, your life will be a blessing to so many others.

How did her faith affect her family?

Her faith affected her mother-in-law. By choosing to be with Naomi, Ruth was able to provide for her mother-in-law. She constantly listened and took Naomi's advice, resulting in a beautiful marriage and baby boy. Ruth not only kept Naomi's husband's and son's names alive, but she also gave her a great legacy that lived on to Jesus Christ.

Her faith affected her husband Boaz. By being a virtuous woman, she was a crown to him when they married (see Prov. 12:4). Though he was older, she presented a son to him that preserved his name.

Our Personal Prayer

Dear Jesus, thank You for being the greatest Friend we could ever have. By dying on the cross for us, You gave us the ultimate example of true friendship. Help us to show the gift of friendship to others that You have shown to us.

Questions to Consider

1. Can you think of someone who needs your offer of friendship?

   _____

   _____

2. What are some characteristics you need to improve to be a virtuous woman?

   _____

   _____

3. What tools are you using to build your house?

   _____

   _____

4. How can you strengthen your friendship with the Lord?

   _____

   _____

Chapter Ten

Four Women Whose Choices Brought Results

I have many choices I need to make every day; and whether or not you realize it, you do, too. While some of our choices are small, like what we should eat for breakfast, others can be big, like should we consider marrying that guy. Either way, our small or big choices bring results.

Since choices bring results, how can we make our choices honor the Lord? Successful choices are made when we base them on principles from God's Word; choices that will not succeed happen when we base them on our emotions and selfish desires.

Four women who made some bad choices that brought bad results are Dinah, Mrs. Potiphar, Herodias, and Salome. Dinah's curiosity resulted in making a costly mistake; Mrs. Potiphar's eye problem resulted in her living a shame-filled life; Herodias' hard heart resulted in living a life of exile; and Salome's heartless cruelty resulted in a cursed life.

Dinah: Her Curiosity Led to a Costly Mistake
Gen. 34:1-31

Dinah's father, Jacob, pitched the family's tents by a Canaanite city called Shechem. Jacob went to Shechem and paid Hamor, a prince of the land, a hundred pieces of silver for his property (Gen. 33:19). When Dinah moved to Shechem, she was a young teenage lady. Dinah's father had two wives, two concubines, and ten other children; her mother's name was Leah. Born number eleven in the family (before Joseph) and being the only girl made her ten older brothers protective of her.

When Dinah heard there was a Canaanite festival of nature worship happening in Shechem,[43] she wanted to go. "Dinah the daughter of Leah, which she bare unto Jacob, went out to see the daughters of the land" (Gen. 34:1). She probably had been to Shechem before and thought a festival would be harmless.

She couldn't have been more wrong! While partying, she met a guy named Shechem whose father (Hamor) was prince of the country. "And when Shechem the son of Hamor the Hivite, prince of the country, saw her, he took her, and lay with her, and defiled her" (Gen. 34:2).

Stripped of her innocence and purity, Dinah managed to make it home. While her brothers worked in the field, she confided to someone what had happened. When her dad heard the news, he "held his peace until they [his sons] were come" (Gen. 34:5). (How could he seemingly not get upset about what happened to his only daughter?)

Hamor showed up to talk to Jacob. He proposed that Jacob let Dinah marry his son Shechem and that they consider letting their sons and daughters marry each other. Shechem next appeared to talk with Dinah's father and brothers. Jacob's sons listened to him and told him they would consent to the marriage under one condition—all the men of Shechem had to be circumcised. Hamor agreed to the deal and told the men of Shechem what they needed to do. Soon every male was circumcised (Gen. 34:24).

On the third day, Simeon and Levi showed up at Shechem. Knowing the men of Shechem would be sore, they took advantage of the moment and killed every male. They killed Hamor and Shechem, took Dinah out of Shechem's house, and took all the spoil from the city (money, animals, women, children, and whatever else they wanted). Jacob told his two sons he was unhappy with what they did, for now their families' reputation had been scarred. I wonder if Dinah felt a little guilty, knowing it all started from a little bit of curiosity.

Dinah's curiosity led to sneakiness. She didn't tell anyone she was going to Shechem and going alone. Her sneakiness led to disobeying. We don't read about her asking permission to go. Do you see the pattern? Curiosity led to sneakiness; sneakiness led to disobedience; disobedience led to losing her purity.

Beware of being curious about things of the world. Your curiosity may lead you to sin. What may seem harmless in the beginning can be very harmful in the end. You may say, "Oh, ____ [you fill in the blank] is just a little thing. Nothing bad will come of it." But remember "a little leaven [choice of sin] leaveneth the whole lump [result]" (Gal. 5:9). Baby steps going in the wrong direction will eventually take you the wrong way.

Don't dabble in anything in which you are unsure. Be careful of your social networking when on the computer. Don't participate in chat rooms, and don't look at sites that appear questionable. When in doubt, don't! 1 Thessalonians 5:22 says we are to "abstain from all appearance of evil"—notice not from evil, but from what appears to be wrong.[44] On things that you are unsure about, you will need to use the Bible's principles as your map and the Holy Spirit as your guide.

Mrs. Potiphar: Her Eyes Affected Her Heart
Gen. 39:7-20

Potiphar purchased a Jewish young man named Joseph from the Ishmaelites to be his slave. As the captain of the guard for the pharaoh of Egypt, Potiphar's job was to protect the pharaoh. Because of his busy schedule, Potiphar made Joseph around his house and observed he was a hard worker. He noticed "the LORD was with him, and that the LORD made all that he did to prosper in his hand" (Gen. 39:3). Potiphar quickly put Joseph in charge of his house and possessions.

"And it came to pass from the time that he had made him overseer in his house, and over all that he had, that the LORD blessed the Egyptian's house for Joseph's sake; and the blessing of the LORD was upon all that he had in the house, and in the field" (Gen. 39:5). Potiphar trusted Joseph so much that he didn't even know what he owned; all he knew was that he had bread to eat!

Joseph was handsome looking, and his prosperity was noticed by Mrs. Potiphar. Then she "*cast her eyes upon Joseph* (italics mine); and she said, Lie with me" (Gen. 39:7). Joseph refused her offer, explaining Potiphar trusted him and that he could not sin against God. Mrs. Potiphar spoke temptingly to Joseph "day by day" (Gen. 39:10), but her attempts were useless.

When Joseph was the only man in her house, she aggressively caught him by his garment, but he ran off—leaving his jacket in her hands! Feeling humiliated, she complained and blamed her husband to the men of the house (they must have heard her hysterics and come back in). She said, "See, he [Potiphar] hath brought in an Hebrew unto us to mock us; he came in unto me to lie with me, and I cried with a loud voice" (Gen. 39:14).

Mrs. Potiphar took Joseph's coat and laid it by her side until her husband came home. After criticizing Potiphar's decision to hire Joseph, she accused Joseph of threatening her (Gen. 39:17-18). Potiphar was upset when he heard this, but it appears he was angry with his wife and not Joseph. Remember, Potiphar is captain of the guard—and the penalty for a servant to commit adultery with his wife would be death. Instead, he sent Joseph to jail. Joseph later was made second in command of Egypt by Pharaoh; I wonder what she thought every time she saw him, this time with Joseph being her superior?

Once Mrs. Potiphar "cast her eyes on Joseph," she was going to let nothing stop her from getting what she wanted. Don't underestimate the power your eyes have over you! Jesus knows the power one eyeball has over your body. He said, "And if thine eye offend thee, pluck it out: it is better for thee to enter into the kingdom of God with one eye, than having two eyes to be cast into hell fire" (Mark 9:47).

What our eyes see our hearts will feel. Jeremiah said, "Mine eye affecteth mine heart" (Lam. 3:51). A good step in keeping a clean heart is to put godly things before our eyes. "Open thou mine eyes, that I may behold wondrous things out of thy law" (Ps. 119:18).

98

For us to keep our hearts clean it is vital we guard what our eyes watch. "I will set no wicked thing before mine eyes [choice]... a froward heart shall depart from me [result]" (Ps. 101:3-4).

Herodias: Her Hard Heart Rejected God's Word
Mark 6:17-28

Marriage to her Uncle Philip bored Herodias. Because Philip's father, Herod the Great, had disinherited him, Philip was just a private citizen of Rome. When Philip's powerful brother Herod Antipas came to visit them in Rome, she and Herod Antipas began an adulterous affair.[45] Herod was also married to the daughter of Aretas, king of Arabia.

Herod and Herodias divorced their spouses to marry each other. Aretas, Herod's father-in-law, was so mad about the divorce that he attacked Herod and nearly destroyed his army![46] Power-hungry Herodias knew her marriage to Herod Antipas would definitely put her in the political spotlight. Her daughter Salome (by her husband Philip) lived with them.

Herodias couldn't understand why Herod would "gladly" listen to a man named John the Baptist (Mark 6:20). When John confronted them regarding their divorce and remarriage, Herod no longer "gladly" heard them. Herodias argued with John, wishing she had the power to kill him (Mark 6:19).

Instead, she urged Herod to immediately put John in the prison of Machaerus. "For Herod himself had sent forth and laid hold upon John, and bound him in prison *for Herodias' sake*" (italics mine) (Mark 6:17). When Herod's birthday party came, Herodias saw her chance to get rid of John. Knowing her husband's actions when intoxicated by alcohol, it was probably Herodias' idea for her daughter Salome to dance a sensual dance. After Salome's erotic dance, Herod granted her a wish. When Salome asked Herodias, "What shall I ask?" Herodias quickly said, "The head of John the Baptist" (Mark 6:24).

After John's beheading, Herodias' family's problems never went away. Because Herod's conscience troubled him, when he heard accounts of Jesus, he was convinced Jesus was John risen from the dead (Mark 6:16). History states that Herod, due to his wife's nagging, demanded to be given the title of king by the Roman emperor. This move backfired and as a result he and Herodias were banished to France![47]

Though Herodias heard John the Baptist speak with her ears, she chose to not listen with her heart. "But they refused to hearken, and pulled away the shoulder, and stopped their ears, that they should not hear. Yea, *they made their hearts as an adamant stone* (italics mine), lest they should hear the law, and the words which the LORD of hosts hath sent in his spirit by the former prophets: therefore came a great wrath from the LORD of hosts" (Zech. 7:11-12).

Based on these two verses we will notice three signs of a person with a cold heart. She will reject God's Word; her body language will indicate her refusal to listen; she will choose to harden her heart from God's Word. All these will result in "great wrath" from the Lord. "He that hardeneth his heart [a choice] shall fall into mischief [result]" (Prov. 28:14).

Since we do all we can to make sure our heart is physically strong, shouldn't we as Christians make it a priority to keep our heart spiritually tender for the Lord?

Salome: Her Cruelty Brought a Curse on Her Head
Mark 6:17-28

Salome, Herodias' daughter, came from the power-hungry family of Herod. Her great-grandpa was Herod the Great, the man who sought to kill Jesus when he was a baby and killed hundreds of other babies. Murder, hatred, adultery...these characterize the family Salome was brought up in.

When Salome's step-father, Herod, started planning his birthday, she was very excited. She knew many important men and high government officials were invited to his party (Mark 6:21). Perhaps she saw this as her chance to shine in front of a bunch of men. During the party, she came out and sensually danced before them. Her dancing pleased Herod and the other men very much. Herod promised he would give whatever she asked, even if it were half his kingdom (Mark 6:23).

What a decision! Knowing her mother would help her decide, she asked Herodias what she should request. Her mother told her to ask for John the Baptist's head. "And she came in straightway with haste unto the king, and asked, saying, I will that thou give me by and by in a charger the head of John the Baptist" (Mark 6:24-25). "By and by" meant she immediately wanted his head, and wanted it in a "charger" or on a platter.

"And the king was exceeding sorry; yet for his oath's sake, and for their sakes which sat with him, he would not reject her" (Mark 6:26). Was Herod sorry because he had to kill John? No. It was his fear of the people rioting and "jeopardizing his political interests that upset him."[48]

According to Josephus, Salome lived long enough to be married twice and had three children. An image of her with her second husband, Aristobulus, was even imprinted on three kinds of Roman coins. Tradition says she died by falling through sharp ice, resulting in her head being cut off by the ice![49] (Was her neck required by the Lord in exchange for John the Baptist's neck?)

Salome's life has been portrayed in numerous plays, operas, poems, films, and even in a 2009 realistic video game! The video game depicts Salome cutting off John the Baptist's head. Isn't this AWFUL? She is being exalted for her cruelty! Yet, we see her cruelty put a curse on her own head.

What a cruel person does not realize is that the person he hurts the most is himself. "The merciful man doeth good to his own soul: but he that is cruel troubleth his own flesh" (Prov. 11:17). When Simeon and Levi were cruel to the men of Shechem, they were cursed by their father on his deathbed. "Cursed be their anger, for it was fierce; and their wrath, for it was cruel" (Gen. 49:7).

How can we put blessings on our head? "And it shall come to pass, if thou shalt hearken diligently unto the voice of the LORD thy God, to observe and to do all his commandments which I command thee this day [a choice], that the LORD thy God will set thee on high above

101

all nations of the earth: And all these blessings shall come on thee, and overtake thee [result], if thou shalt hearken unto the voice of the LORD thy God" (Deut. 28:1-2).

A Lesson to Learn from These Four Women

There's bad and good news from these women. The bad news is when you make a choice to fulfill your selfish desires, it's hard to rebound. Can God have mercy when we make bad choices? YES. Even when we goof up, God can still choose to use us and help get us out of our mess. An example is Peter. He chose to deny his Lord, but after he repented, God chose him to be a great leader for the Christian movement. If you have made some bad choices, confess them before the Lord and start turning the pages of your Bible to help you with your upcoming choices.

The good news is when you base your choices on principles of God's Word, you will reap good results. "Say ye to the righteous [saved people who choose to do right], that it shall be well with him: for they shall eat the fruit of their doings [result]" (Is. 3:10-11).

And lastly, remember this—you are not alone; the Lord is with you and His Spirit indwells in you. He will help you with the choices you need to make. As you are faced with countless choices to make every day, remember to listen to Him. He will always be there to help you.

How did their faith affect their family?

Dinah's faith affected her parents and brothers. "Dinah's mistake and Shechem's sin not only affected them. Dinah's whole family became involved and suffered reproach."[50]

Mrs. Potiphar's faith affected her husband and household. How could her husband live in anything but defeat after this episode? When they lost Joseph as overseer of their house and field, they lost out on blessings, too.

Herodias' faith affected her husband Herod. Her influence kept Herod from ever listening to John and from Jesus. Later, Herod would mock and persecute Jesus (Luke 23:11). It was her idea for Herod to ask the title of king, causing her and Herod to forever be in exile. Her faith affected her daughter Salome. Due to her influence in Salome's life, it was to Herodias that Salome went and inquired what she should ask of Herod.

Salome's faith affected her mother, step-father, husbands, and children. After her erotic dance, she became a symbol as a female seductress. Choosing John's death resulted in Jesus leaving the area. Many people could have been blessed by Jesus, but Salome was responsible for driving Him away.

Our Personal Prayer

Lord, You know all the choices we are faced with making every day. Please give us the wisdom we need to make wise choices. Help us to stay in Your Word so that we can make good choices for You.

Questions to Consider

1. Is there something you are curious about that you need to determine to not to think about?_____

_____

2. How can your eyes affect your heart?_____

_____

3. Based on Luke 6:49, what will happen to someone who hears God's Word but will not do it?

_____

_____

4. What are some choices you can make for the Lord that will bring blessings in your life?

_____

_____

Women Who Needed Wisdom before Their Crisis and One Who Used Her Wisdom for Her Crisis

You never know when you need to have wisdom before a crisis. Ask God for wisdom before a crisis happens instead of waiting. When Solomon became king of Israel, the Lord told Solomon to ask what he wanted. New to the throne, yet not in the midst of a crisis, Solomon wanted wisdom for what lay ahead. He didn't ask to have wisdom later; instead, he said, "Give me now wisdom" (2 Chron. 1:10).

There's nothing wrong with asking for wisdom in the middle of a crisis. "If any of you lack wisdom, let him ask of God, that giveth to all men liberally, and upbraideth not; and it shall be given him" (James 1:5). In context, this verse is talking about asking God for wisdom when trials occur. However, let's take this lesson a step further and seek wisdom before something happens. Wisdom won't prevent troubles from coming, but it will help you know what to do when a crisis happens.

In this lesson, the first four women needed wisdom before their crisis. In Solomon's story, neither of the two women was named; I will refer to one mother as the true mother. In the story about the famine, one mother is called the foolish mother. The last woman is the wise woman of Abel, who acted on her wisdom.

Teach Others to Get Wisdom
1 Kings 3:16-28

While King David was on his deathbed, he gave advice to his son Solomon. "And keep the charge of the LORD thy God, to walk in his ways, to keep his statues, and his commandments, and his judgments, and his testimonies, as it is written in the law of Moses, that thou mayest prosper in all that thou doest...Do therefore according to thy wisdom" (1 Kings 2:3, 6). David knew his son would need wisdom in life.

Solomon's responsibilities were huge—he was the new king of a nation and a new husband. One night, after Solomon had offered to the Lord a thousand sacrifices, God appeared in a dream to Solomon and said, "Ask what I shall give thee" (2 Chron. 1:7). Solomon said, "Give me now wisdom and knowledge, that I may go out and come in before this people: for who can judge this thy people, that is so great?" (2 Chron. 1:10).

"Because this was in [his] heart" (2 Chron. 1:11), his answer pleased the Lord. God reassured Solomon that not only would he have wisdom and understanding, but also wealth and honor. Solomon woke up from the dream and headed to Jerusalem, ready to worship the Lord and to serve his people.

Shortly afterward, Solomon needed to use his wisdom. Two women and a baby were at the palace fighting over who was the true mother. The two were harlots, not respectable ladies. "It is probable the cause had been heard in the inferior courts, before it was brought before Solomon, and had been found special, the judges being unable to determine it."[51] Because Solomon's father influenced him to get wisdom from the Lord, Solomon would be able to solve the case of the mystery mother.

In Proverbs 4:3-9, Solomon says David stressed the importance of getting wisdom. "He taught me also, and said unto me...Get wisdom, get understanding...Wisdom is the principal thing; therefore get wisdom...She shall give to thine head an ornament of grace: a crown of glory shall she deliver to thee" (Prov. 4:4, 5, 7, 9). David knew that a crown of wisdom was the best crown for a king to wear.

We always praise Solomon for asking wisdom from the Lord, but let's remember it was David who planted the seed thought in Solomon's heart that he needed wisdom. Are you mentoring anyone or do you have any children? Emphasize to them their need for wisdom and explain it's even better to get than gold (Prov. 16:16). Reading a chapter of Proverbs a day and memorizing verses on wisdom will be a help.

Always point someone to the Lord; if they don't know Him as their Savior, they won't realize He is the source of wisdom. A lady must first have a fear of the Lord before she can get wisdom from Him. "Give instruction to a wise man, and he will be yet wiser: teach a just man, and he will increase in learning. The fear of the LORD is the beginning of wisdom" (Prov. 9:9-10a). Like a flower gives honey to a bee, teach wisdom to those who are buzzing around you.

Your Wisdom Should Help Others See the Lord

As the women stood before King Solomon, the true mother boldly told the story. She explained that she and the other mother were roommates and had been due to have their babies born about the same time. She had her baby first, and then three days later the other mother had her baby. No one else was present at either of the births, and each woman must have helped deliver her roommate's baby.

She continued: "And this woman's child died in the night; because she overlaid it. And she arose at midnight, and took my son from beside me, while thine handmaid slept, and laid it in her bosom, and laid her dead child in my bosom. And when I rose in the morning to give my child suck, behold, it was dead: but when I had considered it in the morning, behold, it was not my son, which I did bear" (1 Kings 3:19-21).

The other woman couldn't be silent any longer. "Nay; but the living is my son, and the dead is thy son" (1 Kings 3:22). The true mother quickly disagreed and was silenced by King Solomon. "Then said the king, The one saith, This is my son that liveth, and thy son is the dead: and the other saith, Nay; but thy son is the dead, and my son is the living" (1 Kings 3:23).

After ordering that a sword be brought, King Solomon said, "Divide the living child in two, and give half to the one, and half to the other" (1 Kings 3:25). Upon hearing this, the true mother felt compassion and love for her baby and said, "O my lord, give her the living child, and

107

in no wise slay it" while the other lady said, "Let it be neither mine nor thine, but divide it" (1 Kings 3:26).

The king immediately discerned the true mother to be the right mother and ordered, "Give her the living child, and in no wise slay it: she is the mother thereof" (1Kings 3:27). How relieved the true mother was that her king was such a wise man! When word spread about King Solomon's wise decision, the people of Israel "feared the king: for they saw that the wisdom of God was in him, to do judgment" (1 Kings 3:28). Solomon's wisdom was not wasted; he helped others see the Lord.

Solomon's wisdom was spread not only throughout his kingdom but also to other parts of the world as well (1 Kings 4:30-34).When the Queen of Sheba, ruler of people in the southern part of Arabia, "heard of the fame of Solomon *concerning the name of the LORD* (italics mine)" (1 Kings 10:1), she traveled to visit Solomon to see if everything she heard was true. After realizing she hadn't even heard the half of it, she blessed Solomon's Lord. "Blessed be the LORD thy God" (1 Kings 10:9).

Everything we receive from the Lord should be used to help others know Him. When Stephen stood before the religious rulers, they were unable "to resist the wisdom and the spirit by which he spake" (Acts 6:10). The great leader Moses "was learned in all the wisdom of the Egyptians, and was mighty in words and in deeds" (Acts 7:22).

Wisdom is not meant to be bottled up. "The words of a man's mouth are as deep waters, and the wellspring of wisdom as a flowing brook" (Prov. 18:4). A wise person will speak wise words and like a gentle stream will flow and help others.

Your Foolishness Is Observed by Others
2 Kings 6:24-33

Times were tough for the people in Samaria. The king of Syria, whose country was north of Israel, "gathered all his host, and went up, and besieged Samaria" (2 Kings 6:24). To make matters worse, Samaria was going through a famine. The quality and prices of food were outrageous! "An ass's head was sold for fourscore pieces of silver, and the fourth part of a cab of dove's dung for five pieces of silver" (2 Kings 6:25). (A fourth part of a cab may have been one or two pints.[52]) Paying a high price to eat the head of a donkey, an unclean animal, indicated how desperate the people were.

In Samaria lived two mothers who, along with their sons, were starving to death. One day, the foolish mother was approached by another mother with a horrendous suggestion. "Give thy son, that we may eat him *to day* (italics mine), and we will eat my son tomorrow" (2 Kings 6:28). What a shocking proposal—and even more shocking is the foolish mother agreed to do this!

She didn't bother to think about it; she just knew she was dying to eat some food and get her belly full. So, along with the other mother, she boiled her son ("it was obviously not a grown child"[53]) and they ate him!

On the next day, the foolish mother went to the other mother and said, "Give thy son, that we may eat him" (2 Kings 6:29). Instead of the other mother following through with her part of the deal, she backed out! She didn't want to kill her son and instead "hid" him (2 Kings 6:29). Her trickiness made the foolish mother angry!

When she saw the king walk by, she cried, "Help, my lord, O king" (2 Kings 6:26). King Jehoram said, "If the LORD do not help thee, whence shall I help thee?...What aileth thee?" (2 Kings 6:27-28). After she told him how the other mother tricked her, the king was upset, but not at her. Thinking this was the prophet Elisha's fault, he went to Elisha and said, Why "should I wait for the LORD any longer?" (2 Kings 6:33).

Elisha informed the king that there would be an over-abundant amount of food available for tomorrow; so much, in fact, that flour and barley would be sold for cheap prices. True to his word, God miraculously provided the food as Elisha said (for a great story read chapter seven). If that foolish woman had not made a hasty decision based on her feelings, her son would have been alive.

The foolish mother had a reputation of being foolish; why else would the tricky mother know who to approach with such a shocking proposal? If the foolish mother had been known as a wise mother, the tricky mother wouldn't have even dared suggest what she did. Proverbs 9:13 says a foolish woman is clamorous, meaning loud. Since a foolish woman is loud, she is the one to proclaim her own foolishness.

You can't hide your foolishness; people know what kind of person you are. People will also know if you are foolish enough to go along with their foolish ideas or if you are wise enough to do what is right. One way to avoid being foolish is to avoid associating with foolish people (Prov. 14:7). I'm not saying you are never to be *with* a foolish person, because you need to be soul winning and mentoring others; I am saying you should not hang out with a foolish person. A wise person will spend time with wise people.

"Every wise woman buildeth her house" (Prov. 14:1). This is not referring to an actual house structure but to what is being built in the hearts of those in your home. Just like you see what kind of house is being built down the street, your friends and family will see what kind of a house you are building for your family. If you are a wise person, your wisdom will be obvious to others.

You Need Wisdom for Today
1 Sam. 21:16-22

It was a time of political unrest for the nation of Israel. After his son Absalom's rebellion, King David needed to re-establish his claim to the throne. A man named Sheba, from the tribe of Benjamin like former King Saul, seized this opportunity to start a revolt against King David. "So every man of Israel [mostly from the northern tribe] went up from after David, and followed Sheba" (2 Sam. 20:2). Joab, David's general, pursued Sheba to the city of Abel.

Abel was an important city in Israel; its reputation was to have wise people living there and to help give advice to those with problems or questions. After a wise woman heard an army approach and try to batter down their wall (2 Sam. 20:15), she instantly knew what to do.

110

"Then cried a wise woman out of the city, Hear, hear; say, I pray you, unto Joab, Come near hither, that I may speak with thee" (2 Sam. 20:16). Joab approached, and she said, "Art thou Joab? And he answered, I am he. Then she said unto him, Hear the words of thine handmaid. And he answered, I do hear" (2 Sam. 20:17). How interesting that this general of an army is no longer in control; instead, he is listening to a woman!

Despite the fact this wise woman knew Joab's reputation to be a bloodthirsty warrior, she was not afraid. After reminding him the people of Abel were known for their wisdom, she said, "I am one of them that are peaceable and faithful in Israel: thou seekest to destroy a city and a mother in Israel: why wilt thou swallow up the inheritance of the LORD?" (2 Sam. 20:19). In other words, she questioned his failure to follow the law in Deuteronomy 20:10 that stated, "When thou comest nigh unto a city to fight against it, then proclaim peace unto it."

Seeing the wisdom in her words, Joab answered "Far be it, far be it from me, that I should swallow up or destroy" (2 Sam. 20:20). Then Joab explained that Sheba was a threat to King David and to the throne. She instantly told him, "Behold, his head shall be thrown to thee over the wall" (2 Sam. 20:21)! "Then the woman went unto all the people *in her wisdom* (italics mine). And they cut off the head of Sheba...and cast it out to Joab" (2 Sam. 20:22). Satisfied, Joab and his army left the city of Abel to inform King David the threat to his reign was over.

Though a gruesome story, the wise woman ended the war and prevented many people from being killed. Notice that when Joab told her Sheba was in the city, she knew what to say and said it; she didn't ask him to give her five minutes to think about the situation. Like her, you may face a situation where you won't have time to pray or seek counsel. Would you react with wisdom in a crisis that was happening too fast?

Ultimately, how you react in a crisis will be determined by what you are doing with the rest of your time.[54] If you are in the habit of praying and reading your Bible day in and day out, the Holy Spirit will bring to your memory the right words to say. Like the wise woman who knew the Holy Scriptures to mention the law to Joab, are you familiar with your Bible to know what it says?

Teddy Roosevelt, a former President of the United States, once said: Nine-tenths of wisdom consists in being wise in time.[55] What good would wisdom do you if you used it too late?

A Lesson to Learn from These Women

Notice the references in this chapter from the book of Proverbs. Did you know that it was Solomon, the wisest man in the world, who wrote the majority of those proverbs? If you want to have a good start in wisdom, read and apply the words of advice Solomon had to say.

A crisis revealed each of these women's character, and their character was formed by their everyday lifestyle. Realize that what you do on a daily basis will affect what you will do in a crisis. The wise woman of Abel not only had wisdom, but she also had an active wisdom—she knew what to say, what to do, and how to do it. If a crisis came today, would you have wisdom to know what to say or do?

How did their faith affect their family?

The true mother's faith affected her baby boy. Her willingness to give him up is what brought her son back to her.

The foolish mother's faith affected her son. She killed him to satisfy her hunger.

The wise woman of Abel's faith affected her whole family by saving the lives of everyone who lived in Abel.

Our Personal Prayer

Lord, we know that only You know what lies ahead in our paths. Please give us wisdom today so that we can make wise choices for You today.

Questions to Consider

1. Who could you start teaching wisdom to, and what steps do you
   need to take to begin?

   _____

   _____

2. In Luke 21:15, how are the mouth and wisdom connected?

   _____

   _____

3. Would the Lord view you as a foolish or a wise person when you
   are going through a crisis? What about your friends and family?

   _____

   _____

4. What do you need to do today to help you obtain wisdom?

   _____

   _____

Chapter Twelve

Sapphira

A Woman Whose Sin Affected Her Church Family

Acts 5:1-11

A church is more than a building or program; it's a gathering of believers of Jesus Christ. Inhabited by the Holy Spirit, the people gather united as the body of Christ (1 Cor. 12:12-13, 27). Just like your body is made up of different parts (hands, ears, eyes), the church as one body has "many members" (1 Cor. 12:20).

When all the "members" of the body of Christ are Spirit-filled (meaning Spirit controlled), there will be sweet unity in the church. By the same meaning, when some "members" are controlled by their sins, this can seriously damage the church (1 Cor. 12:26). Sin interrupts the victory of God's people.

Sapphira, along with her husband Ananias, had some secret sins—greediness, selfishness, lies, hypocrisy—which the Lord swiftly punished. His judgment was necessary to preserve the unity of their church in Jerusalem.

An Inward Desire for the Praise of Man

It was a new age—the age of a new church, a new covenant (where we get the word testament), and the Holy Spirit. The veil from the temple had been rent from the top to bottom when Jesus died on the cross, symbolizing full fellowship with God was now available.

As Satan watched thousands of people put their trust in Jesus, he thought maybe persecution would quench the fire of Christianity's flame (Acts 4:1-3). But he was wrong; like fans to a flame, the persecution caused Christianity to wildly sweep through the whole region (Acts 4:4). To put out the fire of this explosive movement, Satan knew he would have to put the fire out at its base; he would destroy the church by destroying the families within the church.

Being part of the new church in the town of Jerusalem was very exciting for Sapphira and her husband, Ananias. Their pastor, the apostle Peter, was an amazing man. He had, through the power of God, healed a lame man and also preached incredible sermons where about eight thousand people were saved (Acts 2:41, 4:4)! Life certainly wasn't boring at their church.

Excitement about the work of the Lord rapidly spread among the Christians, and soon the people desired to financially help those with needs (Acts 4:32-34). People started to sell their homes and land and lay the money at the apostles' feet. Then, the apostles would distribute the money to those who had needs (Acts 4:35).

During one particular church service, as Sapphira sat with Ananias, she saw a man named Barnabas receive praise for giving lots of money to the apostles. Like others, he, too, had sold his home and had given all the money to the church. Sapphira noticed the open admiration he received from the people. Perhaps, as they left church that night, she heard people talk about Barnabas' sacrificial gift. In her heart, she wished she would someday receive praise in front of others like Barnabas did. She liked the idea of looking special and important in front of her friends.

No doubt, Barnabas' praise was the main topic she and Ananias talked about as they went home that night. Sapphira knew that Ananias also desired to be praised like Barnabas. Instead of praising God for the exciting things happening in their church, they were more concerned about looking good to others. Because their hearts were full of pride, they were thinking only of themselves.

Are you obsessed with wanting to receive praise from people? Do you feel depressed if no one compliments you for something? Do you envy those who appear to constantly get streams of compliments? If so, this is a matter of pride, for you are thinking only of yourself. Pride doesn't come from your heavenly Father, but from the devil. "For all that is in the world, the lust of the flesh, and the lust of the eyes, and the pride of life, is not of the Father, but is of the world" (1 Jn. 2:16).

It is recorded that many chief rulers believed in Jesus, but because they were afraid of what some other men would think and do, they did not "confess him" to be their Savior (John 12:42). Why? "For they loved the praise of men more than the praise of God" (John 12:43). It is a proud person who will not get saved because he doesn't want to be looked down upon.

Loving the praise of man will only bring personal destruction. The praise of man leads to pride, which then will hinder the work of God. "If praise of man becomes a foothold in your heart it will corrupt your character and service."[56] If you desire the praise of man, confess this as a sin of pride. Your desire should only be to receive praise from God, and God alone.

An Evil Plan Conceived

Maybe that was the night Ananias and Sapphira talked about selling their land. Yet, because they were greedy in heart, they knew they couldn't give all the money away. Because they wanted the praise and admiration of the people so badly, they knew it must *appear* that they had given sacrificially.

Soon their plan had begun to form. After giving plenty of money to the apostles, they would keep back the rest of the money. They would look good on the outside to their friends and still have plenty of money for themselves. Sapphira may have felt a little guilty about this, but her desire for wanting praise consumed her more than doing the right thing.

Let us use our imagination with what happened next. When Sapphira found out they had a buyer for the house, she was ecstatic! She and Ananias headed to the title office to sign the closing papers of the land, feeling very important. She knew it would be a pain to move out of the house (or maybe it was an extra house?). After the waiting period of their house being in escrow, they found out from the real estate agent everything was all set to go. She and Ananias received their check from the buyer and quickly took off to the bank to cash it. After they arrived at home, they distributed the money into two piles, one for the apostles and the other pile for themselves.

"It is bad to do mischief on a sudden thought, much worse to do it with design and forethought."[57] By planning something evil, you are pushing aside the guidance of the Holy Spirit; you are listening only to yourself and not to your God. You are practicing how to be an awful Christian when you quench the Holy Spirit's working in your heart. With the Holy Spirit's working in your heart quenched, Satan is the one who will fill the space (Acts 5:3).

Conceiving an evil plan will start from the heart. Later on, Peter asked Ananias why he conceived the plan in his heart (Acts 5:4). Conceiving something evil in the heart will only spring up bad roots. "Then when lust hath conceived, it bringeth forth sin: and sin, when it is finished, bringeth forth death" (James 1:15).

Instead of planning to do evil, plan to do good. "But mercy and truth shall be to them that devise good" (Prov. 14:22). One good plan would be to find out how you can be a blessing to others in your church. Be on the lookout for how you can serve someone. Does someone need encouraging? Is there someone you could invite for dinner? Is there a burden the pastor's wife has that you could shoulder? Plan to be a blessing to others, and don't be surprised if you're the one who ends up blessed!

A Gift of Leftovers to God

Sapphira and Ananias were thrilled at their good fortune! Maybe Sapphira already started to imagine the church service where she would be applauded by her friends, and her husband would suddenly be someone important. Probably, Ananias went over the details of the story with Sapphira so that if she were questioned about the money, she would know what to say.

They certainly didn't want their plan to be revealed to anybody, especially now that they were getting close to their goal. Though they knew they could have just told the truth and given half of the money to the apostles, they didn't want to. Because they wanted the praise of man more than the praise of God, they wanted everyone to believe they had given sacrificially.

Before Ananias left, I'm sure they said their good-byes and "good lucks." Ananias headed to the church with the money designated for the church (Acts 5:1). Perhaps Sapphira decided to do some shopping with the leftover money.

Ananias quickly went on his way. Surely He was eager to start getting some "pats of praises" on his back. He brought his and Sapphira's "certain part, and laid it at the apostles' feet" (Acts 5:2). Instead of seeing Peter's smiling face, he saw Peter looking soberly at him. Peter said, "Ananias, why hath Satan filled thine heart to lie to the Holy Ghost, and to keep back part of the price of the land? Whiles it remained, was it not thine own? and after it was sold, was it not in thine own power? why hast thou conceived this thing in thine heart? thou hast not lied unto men, but unto God" (Acts 5:3-4).

"And Ananias hearing these words fell down, and gave up the ghost: and great fear came on all them that heard these things. And the young men arose, wound him up, and carried him out, and buried him" (Acts 5:5-6). Sapphira's husband, her partner-in-crime, had died a terrible death as judgment from the Lord! It was shocking, yet why would God bless anybody who would lie and only give God the leftovers?

God doesn't need our money for His business. What He needs is willing, eager people with willing hearts. He truly does own the cattle on a thousand hills, but does He own your heart's desires? Giving is not a matter of making sure God will have the funds that He needs. Giving is an attitude. When was the last time you ever got excited about giving to God?

Matthew 6:24 says, "No man can serve two masters: for either he will hate the one, and love the other; or else he will hold to the one, and despise the other. Ye cannot serve God and mammon [money]." You can only serve one. Which one are you serving?

You may claim to not have enough money to pay your bills and give money to God. Yet, do you have enough money to satisfy your entertainment? Do you have enough money for unnecessary luxuries like high speed internet, lattes from Starbucks, manicures, travel, clothing accessories? If you have money for these but don't give to God, you are not serving God; He is not your master.

To the person who truly wants to give to God, but doesn't think it will make sense, let me challenge you to prove Him. "Bring ye all the tithes into the storehouse, that there may be meat in mine house, and prove me now herewith, saith the LORD of hosts, if I will not open you the windows of heaven, and pour you out a blessing, that there shall not be room enough to receive it" (Mal. 3:10).

God will bless those who give to Him. You may not see the results right away, and your blessings may not be what you had in mind, but He will bless you. "Give, and it shall be given unto you; good measure, pressed down, and shaken together, and running over, shall men give into your bosom" (Luke 6:38).

A Lasting Shame to Her Name

After having been gone for about three hours (Acts 5:7), Sapphira decided to go see what was happening with Ananias at the church. Maybe she imagined the apostles personally had taken Ananias out to lunch. As she headed to the church, she had no idea she was a widow. She had no clue about God's judgment that had taken place in her husband's life.

At last, Sapphira reached the church (Acts 5:7). As she walked in, she probably looked around for Ananias. Instead, she saw Peter. Walking over to Peter, she noticed he was not smiling at her. He asked her, "Tell me whether ye sold the land for so much? And she said, Yea, for so much" (Acts 5:8). She knew what she was supposed to say because she and Ananias had made sure their story would be the same.

How shocked she must have been at Peter's response! "How is that ye have agreed *together* (italics mine) to tempt the Spirit of the Lord? behold, the feet of them which have buried thy husband are at the door, and shall carry thee out" (Acts 5:9). After hearing these terrible words, Sapphira fell over dead at Peter's feet. Instead of casting money at his feet, like other land owners did (Acts 4:37), the only thing she cast was her dead body. With her life now over, she was buried by her husband (Acts 5:10).

The dirt she had been excited about getting money from was the same dirt she ended up being buried in. Sapphira did get the recognition she deserved. The Bible says that "many" heard what happened to her and her husband (Acts 5:11). Definitely being known as a "liar" was not what she had in mind, yet her actions gave her a name.

Your name is more than what you were called the day you were born. Your name involves your reputation, your character—who you really are. "A good name is rather to be chosen than great riches" (Prov. 22:1). Ultimately, it is what God thinks of you that matters; but your name will mean something to people here on earth, as well. May your name be honorable and bring honor to God.

Not only should your name bring honor to God but also to your church family. Have you ever determined what a church was like just because you knew someone who went there? For the good or the bad, we make these conclusions because church members are representatives of their church. Sapphira's name was characterized by her deceit, and it definitely put her church "on the map," so to speak. We will never know until eternity the lasting influence our name can have on many generations to come—so let's make our name a lasting honor instead of a lasting shame!

A Lesson to Learn from Sapphira

God wants holiness in His church. The Holy Spirit wants to move freely in the assembly without the sins of the saints quenching Him. As a member of the body of Christ, and hopefully a member of a church, realize you have a responsibility and accountability to your brothers and sisters in Christ to be a Spirit-filled Christian.

The apostle Paul was very aware of the dangers of a sin-filled church (meaning controlled by sin, and ultimately Satan). He reminded the church at Corinth and Galatia that a "little leaven" (representing sin) in the bread dough will affect the whole lump (1 Cor. 5:6; Gal. 5:9).

Wow! Isn't it amazing how your life can be so affective to others—for the good or for the bad? Plan your life to be a blessing to thousands of others to further the Lord's kingdom. And may your faith have a positive effect in your family and in the family of God.

How did her faith affect her family?

Her faith affected her husband Ananias. Peter mentioned that she and Ananias *together* tempted "the Spirit of the Lord" (Acts 5:9). Together they talked, together they planned. Their prideful hearts were knitted together, resulting in their dead bodies being buried together.

Our Personal Prayer

Lord, we want the Holy Spirit to move freely in our church. Help us to earnestly strive to be a Spirit-filled Christian so that others can feel You working in their hearts. Our desire is to receive praise from You.

Questions to Consider

1. Is your motive for serving the Lord to receive praise from man or praise from God?

   _____

   _____

2. By looking at Proverbs 6:12-19, what are some things a wicked person will do? What does the Lord specifically hate?

_____

_____

3. Are you serving God or your money? What is something you can do to be excited about giving to the Lord?

_____

_____

4. How can you have a positive effect in your church? How is your life affecting your church right now?

_____

_____

God's Plan of Salvation

Are you 100% sure if you died today you would go to Heaven? If not, please take the time to read this carefully. Asking Christ to be your Savior is the most important decision you will ever make—your eternal destination will depend on it. Jesus will only allow those who are saved—those who have asked Him into their heart—into heaven. May the following verses help you to understand you must commit your life today to Jesus Christ.

1. Realize that you are a sinner.

"For all have sinned, and come short of the glory of God" (Romans 3:23).

"As it is written, There is none righteous, no, not one" (Romans 3:10).

2. Understand that because you are a sinner you deserve death.

"For the wages of sin is death; but the gift of God is eternal life through Jesus Christ our Lord" (Romans 6:23).

"Wherefore, as by one man sin entered into the world, and death by sin; and so death passed upon all men, for that all have sinned" (Romans 5:12).

3. Recognize the fact that you must be saved in order to go to heaven.

"Jesus answered and said unto him, Verily, verily, I say unto thee, Except a man be born again, he cannot see the kingdom of God" (John 3:3).

"Not by works of righteousness which we have done, but according to his mercy he saved us" (Titus 3:5).

4. Believe that God loves you so much that He sent His Son, Jesus, to die on the cross for your sin. He conquered death by rising again for you.

"For God so loved the world, that he gave his only begotten Son, that whosoever believeth in him should not perish, but have everlasting life" (John 3:16).

"Who his own self bare our sins in his own body on the tree, that we, being dead to sins, should live unto righteousness: by whose stripes ye were healed" (1 Peter 2:24).

5. Accept Jesus Christ to be your Savior today by believing in your heart and confessing with your mouth.

"That if thou shalt confess with thy mouth the Lord Jesus, and shalt believe in thine heart that God hath raised him from the dead, thou shalt be saved" (Romans 10:9).

"For whosoever shall call upon the name of the Lord shall be saved" (Romans 10:13).

If you believe everything you have read and want to ask Jesus to be your Savior, you can simply pray this right now: "Dear God, I know I'm a sinner. I believe Jesus died on the cross to take my place and that He victoriously arose from the dead. I now ask Him to come into my heart and to be my Savior. Thank you for forgiving me of my sins and giving to me the gift of everlasting life. Amen."

Chapter One: Widow of College Student

[1] Pulpit Commentary, *Sword Searcher* (version 5.5.1.3) [Computer Software]. Broken Arrow, OK: StudyLamp Software LLC, 1995-2009.

[2] Matthew Henry, *Matthew Henry's Commentary*, vol. 2 (Peabody, MA: Hendrickson Publishers, 1991), p. 564.

[3] John G. Butler, *Elisha* (Clinton: LBC Publications, 1992), p. 109.

Chapter Two: Tamar

[4] Charles Ryrie, *Ryrie Study Bible* (Chicago: Moody Publishers, 1994), p. 66.

[5] Jamiesson Fausset Brown, *Sword Searcher* (version 5.5.1.3) [Computer Software]. Broken Arrow, OK: StudyLamp Software LLC, 1995-2009.

[6] John Gill, *Sword Searcher* (version 5.5.1.3) [Computer Software]. Broken Arrow, OK: StudyLamp Software LLC, 1995-2009.

[7] Matthew Henry's Whole Bible Commentary, *Sword Searcher* (version 5.5.1.3) [Computer Software]. Broken Arrow, OK: StudyLamp Software LLC, 1995-2009.

Chapter Three: Four Women Who Gave Their Lives to God's Work

[8] Keith E. Knauss, *Heartbeats of the Holy* (North Fort Meyers, FL: Faithful Life Publishers, 2009), p. 77.

[9] Debi Pearl, *Created to be His Help Meet* (Pleasantville: No Greater Joy, 2004), p. 23.

[10] Dr. Alexander Maclaren, sermon on "Acts," *Precept Austin*, Preceptaustin.org (accessed 2010).

[11] Robert G. Gromacki, *New Testament Survey* (Grand Rapids, MI: Baker Book House, 1974), p. 95.

[12] John G. Butler, *Paul* (Clinton: LBC Publications, 2006), p. 314.

[13] Paul Chappell, *Acts: The Church Alive* (Lancaster, CA: Striving Together Publications, 2006), p. 288.

[14] Robert G. Gromacki, *New Testament Survey* (Grand Rapids, MI: Baker Book House, 1974), p. 185.

[15] Ibid.

[16] Keith E. Knauss, *Heartbeats of the Holy* (North Meyers, FL: Faithful Life Publishers, 2009), p. 77.

[17] Paul Chappell, *Acts: The Church Alive* (Lancaster, CA: Striving Together Publications, 2006), p. 288.

Chapter Four: Jezebel

[18] *Smith's Bible Dictionary* (Uhrichsville, OH: Barbour and Co., Inc., 1987), p. 162.

[19] Ibid.

[20] Smith's Bible Dictionary, *Sword Searcher* (version 5.5.1.3) [Computer Software]. Broken Arrow, OK: StudyLamp Software LLC, 1995-2009.

[21] Wayne Hardy, "Training: More Than Just Obedience," *The Global Baptist Times*, May 2012, p. 2.

Chapter Six: Hannah
[22] Shirley Starr, *Women of the Bible: Helpless and Hurting* (Kearney, NE: Morris Publishing, 2004), p. 44.
[23] Ibid., p. 38.
[24] Pulpit Commentary, *Sword Searcher* (version 5.5.1.3) [Computer Software]. Broken Arrow, OK: StudyLamp Software LLC, 1995-2009.
[25] Matthew Henry's Whole Bible Commentary, *Sword Searcher* (version 5.5.1.3) [Computer Software]. Broken Arrow, OK: StudyLamp Software LLC, 1995-2009.
[26] Terrie Chappell, *It's a Wonderful Life* (Lancaster, CA: Striving Together Publications, 2006), p. 154.

Chapter Seven: Mary
[27] Charles Ryrie, *Ryrie Study Bible* (Chicago: Moody Publishers, 1994), p. 1526.
[28] John MacArthur, sermon on "Luke 2:1-7," Grace to You, www.gty.org (accessed 2012).
[29] Ibid.
[30] *Discipleship*: Prayer (Rochester, NY: First Bible Baptist Church, 2006), lesson 5, p. 2.
[31] Terrie Chappell, *It's a Wonderful Life* (Lancaster, CA: Striving Together Publications, 2006), p. 152.

Chapter Eight: Rebekah
[32] Shirley Starr, *Women of the Bible: Carnal & Conniving* (Kearney, NE: Morris Publishing, 2005), p. 10.
[33] Taken from Lancaster Baptist Church (Lancaster, CA)
[34] John G. Butler, *Jacob* (Clinton: LBC Publications, 1999), p. 47.
[35] Shirley Starr, *Women of the Bible: Carnal and Conniving* (Kearney, NE: Morris Publishing, 2005), p. 13.
[36] John G. Butler, *Jacob* (Clinton: LBC Publications, 1999), p. 52.
[37] Sara Carlson, *Ready or Not* (Murfreesboro, TN: Bill Rice Ranch Publications, 2008), p. 59.
[38] John G. Butler, *Jacob* (Clinton: LBC Publications, 1999), p. 81.
[39] Shirley Starr, *Women of the Bible: Carnal and Conniving* (Kearney, NE: Morris Publishing, 2005), p. 15.
[40] John Butler, *Jacob* (Clinton: LBC Publications, 1999), p. 86.

Chapter Nine: Ruth
[41] Quoted by Tim Larkly
[42] Albert Barnes, *Sword Searcher* (version 5.5.1.3) [Computer Software]. Broken Arrow, OK: StudyLamp Software LLC, 1995-2009.

Chapter Ten: Women Whose Choices Brought Results

[43] Shirley Starr, *Women of the Bible: Helpless and Hurting* (Kearney, NE: Morris Publishing, 2004), p. 11.

[44] Albert Barnes, *Sword Searcher* (version 5.5.1.3) [Computer Software]. Broken Arrow, OK: StudyLamp Software LLC, 1995-2009.

[45] John Butler, *John the Baptist* (Clinton: LBC Publications, 1992), p. 171.

[46] Ibid., p. 173.

[47] Ibid., p. 190.

[48] Ibid., p. 185.

[49] Matthew Henry, *Matthew Henry's Commentary*, vol. 5 (Peabody, MA: Hendrickson Publishers, 1991), p. 201.

[50] Shirley Starr, *Women of the Bible: Helpless and Hurting* (Kearney, NE: Morris Publishing, 2004), p. 15.

Chapter Eleven: Women Who Needed Wisdom before Their Crisis and One Who Used Her Wisdom for Her Crisis

[51] Matthew Henry, *Matthew Henry's Commentary*, vol. 2 (Peabody, MA: Hendrickson Publishers, 1991), p. 464.

[52] Charles Ryrie, *Ryrie Study Bible* (Chicago: Moody Publishers, 1994), p. 596.

[53] John G. Butler, *Elisha* (Clinton: LBC Publications, 1994), p. 254.

[54] David Legge, sermon on "The Woman of Abel," Preach the Word, www.preachtheword.com (accessed 2012).

[55] Ibid.

Chapter Twelve: Sapphira

[56] John G. Butler, *Peter* (Clinton: LBC Publications, 1993), p. 282.

[57] Matthew Henry, *Matthew Henry's Commentary*, vol. 6 (Peabody, MA: Hendrickson Publishers, 1991), p. 45.

Made in United States
Orlando, FL
02 September 2022

21831235R00072